She Is Full of Fire

For permission requests, write to
GCW Publishing House at:
author@thegreatcanadianwoman.ca
Published by GCW Publishing House and Media Group
www.gcwpublishing.com

Quantity sales. Special discounts are available on quantity purchases by corporations, associations, and others.
For details, contact the GCW Publishing House and Media Group head office at the address above.

Paperback 978-1-990370-12-0
eBook ISBN 978-1-990370-13-7

Edited by Christine Stock & Cassie Jeans
Book Designed by Doris Chung
Cover Designed by Michelle Fairbanks
eBook by Ellie Sipilä

Printed in North America

She Is Full of Fire

A collection of real-life stories of women who go against the grain, make hard and unpopular decisions, and live boldly in their personal freedom.

Marika Soleil . Cayman Ferguson . Gaia Carpenter
K.A. Henderson . Kate Ikert . Keli Carpenter
Sharlet Mentes . Shelly Hope . Shae Lemire-Cochrane

SKY EDWARDS

Contents

	Intro	1
One	The Scotsman K.A. Henderson	5
Two	Birth of a Phoenix Cayman Ferguson	25
Three	Ignite, It's an Inside Job Sharlet Mentes	47
Four	Present Over Perfect Marika Soleil	69
Five	My Blind Spot: Why Love Isn't Enough Keli Carpenter	91

Six	Sex, Shame, and Obligation: What It Took to Become Unapologetically Me Gaia Carpenter	**113**
Seven	Running Shelly Hope	**131**
Eight	Lessons Learned Shae Lemire-Cochrane	**149**
Nine	From the Ashes Kate Ikert	**169**
Ten	A Different Kind of Fairy Tale Sky Edwards	**191**
	Final Words	**211**

Bios

K.A. Henderson	24
Cayman Ferguson	45
Sharlet Mentes	67
Marika Soleil	89
Keli Carpenter	111
Gaia Carpenter	130
Shelly Hope	147
Shae Lemire-Cochrane	168
Kate Ikert	189
Sky Edwards	209

Intro

When women come together and share their stories, that's where the magic happens.

As we experience the world and connect with other women through those experiences, the realization that we need this deep honesty, trust, and vulnerability from one another becomes so apparent. This longing to feel understood, seen, and less alone is so profound that without it we feel isolated and lost, along with a ton of other emotions.

When we go through things, we go in search of others who understand. We go in search of information, of stories, of similarities that we can connect to and learn from. We go in search of something more, because we know we need to.

This book holds ten women's lived experiences. They come together to share them with hope of creating that space to connect and grow. These women bear their hearts and share their stories in the most beautiful and vulnerable ways, gifting us insight into their lives and decisions and how they navigated them so that we can learn, connect, and maybe even see bits of ourselves and our stories within their chapters.

We know that no two people experience life the same way, but we all feel and experience some of it in similar ways. These women in this book have proved that, as we see a bit of each of us in each other. We hope that as you read this book, you too, can find bits of yourself woven throughout these pages. We hope you find the sense of connection you are looking for and craving. We hope you can feel the FIRE within these women to not only make these decisions in their own lives but also in the way they share them here, with you. We hope that after reading our stories you can feel that FIRE within yourself, because we all have it, and when we acknowledge it within ourselves, we can begin to help fan it in all those around us.

Chapter One

The Scotsman

K.A. Henderson

It was August 2012. I was a singleton for the first time in ten years. My grandparents, whom I affectionately refer to as Mama and Papa, had the smallest of hunches that I wasn't coping with being alone. After several weeks of wallowing, I received an email from Mama. Someone they had known for many years planned to visit us.

Papa travelled the world as an adviser for sawmills, and Mama would occasionally join him. While working at a mill just outside Dalbeattie, Scotland, Papa met a lovely man and subsequently, his family. Their son, a young (and newly single, as pointed out in Mama's enthusiastic correspondence) Scottish man named Craig was coming for a holiday. He was aspiring to work overseas, and he wanted to see Canada before making his decision. Without hesitation, Mama and Papa offered their home for his lodging. Still overcome by bitterness, I had little interest in spending time with anyone new and didn't even bother searching this

Craig person's name on social media. Later that week, while visiting my parents, I mentioned the email in passing to my mum. I was just making conversation, really. She was curious and asked what he looked like. I honestly didn't know, so we searched for him together. *Well played, Mama. *ADD FRIEND**

I messaged him, endeavouring to sound slightly disinterested, letting him know I was reaching out to him merely because my grandmother thought we should get to know each other before his holiday. I had no idea that this message would completely change the trajectory of my life. We quickly became the best of friends, with a subtle but obvious underlying attraction. The timing, unfortunately, was quite unlucky. We had both recently ended relationships, after all. Still, a bit of harmless flirting never hurt anyone. Within days, however, I was in the thick of a very complicated would-be courtship.

He was the most striking, exotic man ever to be interested in me. It was all very exciting. Still, I couldn't shake the feeling that he was too good to be true and far too good for me. I was never the most popular girl in school, whereas he seemed to be well-liked. He was a confident farm boy; I was a basic city girl. I tried not to compare myself to the superficially glamorous girls in the backgrounds of his social media posts, but a girl can't help but look. It wasn't hard to tell from the photos that some were hoping for his attention, the way they looked at him, eyelashes fluttering. My insecurities skyrocketed. The only way I could keep his attention was through our messages, four thousand miles apart. Those girls were right there in front of him, within reach. I didn't feel like I stood a chance. And yet, every day, he spoke to me.

Each day when I woke, I leaped for my phone to find my good morning message, along with a picture of his view for the day working in the Scottish forests. My heart was so full when I saw that notification. We then spent most of our time chatting about variations between European and North American cars, something we both had an interest in, yet he was far better informed. I spent most of the conversations secretly on search engines, pretending I knew what I was talking about. He was the first person I spoke to every day, and I was the last he spoke to each night. I felt wanted. I felt like I could move on with my life with this gorgeous Scotsman. Still, some days were better than others. Unfortunately, with our distance brought countless misunderstandings, bouts of jealousy, and insecurities. Though he wanted to move on, his past haunted him; he had a relationship that was over, but without closure. There were days when he was cold with me, tortured by it all. Then there were days when I was everything to him—he just wanted to run to me and never look back.

Though I helped Craig navigate the end of this relationship as one of his best friends, it was soul-destroying. At no fault of his, I felt inadequate and unwanted. I must have mattered less to him on those cold days, when I got a few blunt, if any, messages. I wasn't stupid. I knew exactly what was happening. I felt like an option. I was immensely jealous that there were people of influence in his love life within a stone's throw, and I had never even been in the same room as this man. Yet, I was in love with him. There were days I didn't even want to message him to save myself the anxiety and sense of panicked urgency to win him over quickly and completely. I felt dismal, hopeless, with a very real ache in my heart. Still, that heart skipped a beat every time my phone sounded and I lunged for it, hoping it was him.

I didn't even know what Craig sounded like until we spoke for the first time on a video call weeks after those first tumultuous messages. I couldn't understand a word he said. It may have been the poor internet connection. It may have been that I was distracted by his charming Scottish farmhouse hiding behind those beautiful hazel eyes. Most likely, though, it was his gorgeous Scottish accent. As soon as I saw him that day, I was desperate to be with him. In the back of my mind, however, I had that constant niggle: *You're a fool; he is too good for you. He's across the world. He can have anyone, why would he want you?*

We finally met at Calgary airport in October 2012. He was everything I had expected. Tall, broad, bearded, those hazel eyes with a smile all their own as he walked toward me. Our relationship quickly evolved from the strong emotional connection we had made into a physical one. And as one can imagine, our courtship was all but easy. People thought we were ridiculous to be interested in each other from across the world.

A few were jealous. Some were entirely against it, making efforts to stop us. It was both infuriating and frightening. *What if someone talked Craig out of me? Out of us?* Through it all, Craig always told me, "What's for you will not go by you." I loved that about him. Even at our worst, he had this trust in life that it would all work out.

Several months after he had been to Canada, I travelled to Scotland to see him, meet his family, and decide for myself once and for all if all this was worth it. He picked me up at Manchester Airport in May 2013. On the way home, I looked over at him as he was driving and realized I had already come to my decision. I didn't see a life without him.

Two days into my holiday, Craig took me to Edinburgh. Being in that city with him may have been the greatest part of the entire trip. We walked so much those two days that I damaged the nerves in my little toe with my inappropriate footwear. On our first night, we started our evening at a pub with Craig's cousin and his girlfriend. The barman came over and asked if we wanted to do a pub quiz. Before anyone could answer, I blurted out, "Sure!" with great enthusiasm. The man took our quid each, and as he left, I was met with glares and groans. I had no idea pub quizzes took hours and that we had just wasted four quid, as we wouldn't be staying. *Why am I so awkward?!* We had a chuckle, a drink, answered a few of the questions, and headed on our way to our scheduled ghost tour.

I was particularly anxious about the ghost tour. If I am afraid, I like to be held, please and thank you. Craig and I were certainly not at a place of displaying affection. We arrived at the Mercat Cross in the High Street of Edinburgh, and the tour began. The underground was the spookiest part, I would say. Dark, cold, damp, and thick with a presence hard to describe. We were the last tour of the night, so they blew out the candles as we left each room. Complete darkness tickled at the hairs on the back of my neck. Or was there something there? Calm as can be, I quietly hooked Craig's belt loop with my little finger until it was over.

A brisk twilight walk from the cross brought us to Biddy Mulligan's pub in the Grassmarket. It is where I hold the fondest memories of Edinburgh. We were dancing, laughing, and genuinely enjoying each other's company. It was the first time that I actually felt that Craig and I could actually be a couple, and when we were alone, it certainly did feel like we were one. Until it didn't.

Late on our first night in the city, we ordered burgers from a stand on the Royal Mile and sat to eat on some old stone steps. I still couldn't believe I was actually in Scotland and was innocently taking in the scenery while I delicately stuffed my inebriated face. Out of nowhere, Craig slurred to me that he just wasn't ready for a relationship. I remember laughing at him and saying I didn't recall asking. I suppose it had been on his mind. As nonchalant as I acted in response to this unsolicited rejection, I would be lying if I said my heart hadn't broken at that moment. I couldn't get it out of my head for the rest of our time together. *Maybe he simply doesn't want me.*

Back in Dumfries and Galloway, I spent a day with Craig and his stepfather, Donald. Donald was responsible for several thousand sheep that were strategically placed in over two dozen different fields throughout the estate they lived on. They were deworming and ringing lambs in one of the fields. The tiniest ring was stretched thrice its size, wrapped around each lamb's tail and around each male lamb's testes, causing them to fall off after several days. Donald shouted at me to grab one of the lambs for him. It is worth mentioning that at this point, I only understood about 15 percent of what this man said, but I heard this loud and clear. *Who, me?!* He had to be kidding. Craig was watching, standing on a fence with a smirk, so I did it. By that, I mean I chased the little bugger around until I couldn't breathe anymore. He was just close enough to push off balance so I could grab him, fall over in the mud (I hope it was mud), then hold him up to shout triumphantly, "I got it!"; I like to think they cheered for me, but they were laughing. Still, Craig was smiling. This city girl was trying. On the way back to the house, he even stopped the quad for a moment on the forest trail in the pouring rain to give me a kiss. Maybe I was winning him over, but I was out of time.

I woke up on my last morning in Scotland and felt a heaviness. An incredible sadness. I was leaving. I counted down the moments in the car, holding back tears as the Scotland sign came and went. He held my hand for part of the way, which was both reassuring and immensely depressing. Pouring rain was battering the windshield. In an instant, we found ourselves completely stopped on the motorway to Manchester with about forty minutes left in the journey. Needless to say, I missed my flight home. I'd be lying if I said I wasn't slightly relieved that I was still with Craig as the plane soared over us, heading back to Canada without me. I did need to go home at some point, however, so we booked a flight for the following morning and made the two-and-a-half-hour drive home.

We had a perfect evening. Cuddled up on the couch in our sweatpants, we watched TV as the rain trickled down the living room window next to us. I sat for hours listening to the sound of his heart beating, my head resting on his chest. Gentle, strong, and rhythmic, the beating taunted me like the ticking of a clock, time once again running out. The heart that made mine both sing and ache. The heart I wished would just love me.

Unavoidably, we said our goodbyes at the airport in Manchester the following morning. Craig promised me it would only be a couple months until he would be in Canada. I didn't believe him. So much can change in two months. He could change his mind completely, or worse, bring someone with him. I had resigned myself to the thought that we would never be, hugged him tight, and drew in the scent of his neck one last time. I put on a brave face until I got to security. As I looked back once more to see him watching me go, I was sure I would never see him again. The security guard felt bad for me but didn't know what to say. There was nothing he could say. I sat in my middle seat on the plane, tears streaming down my face, staring at my knees. I wanted to disappear.

"He must be some boy," I heard a voice next to me whisper. I looked over, and the woman next to me held out a tissue and smiled. I gave her a weak but appreciative smile in return, accepted the tissue, and gently dabbed my eyes. I felt helpless, hopeless, and despite being in the company of about 249 other people, utterly alone. I felt so heavy I thought the plane surely couldn't leave the runway with the weight of everything inside me. For the entire nine-hour journey home, I stared at the black screen in front of me. I replayed every moment of my time with Craig in Scotland, and his time in Canada, for that matter. *What could I have done differently? How could I have impressed him more?* I realized as the journey home wore on that there was nothing more I could have done. *I was myself. I wore my heart on my sleeve and loved a man with whom I never stood a chance. How can anyone start a relationship from across the world? What WAS I thinking trying to make something like this work? I'm a fool. And now, it's over.*

Three days after I arrived home, after eight of the most difficult and exciting months of my life, I woke up to a message. It was Craig. He told me he had loved me all along. He realized when he got back to his car alone at the airport that he couldn't be without me, and he asked me to be his. This was all I had wanted. Part of me couldn't believe it was happening. *Is he really mine after all we've been through?* Anxiety and pessimism crept in. I still felt it was too good to be true. Something or someone would change his mind, and some did try—showing up on his doorstep, panda eyes from running mascara, begging him not to be with me. It was maddening. Despite my worries, anxieties, and the annoying efforts of a few, as promised, Craig moved to Canada to be with me two months later.

The following summer, due to an oversight with Craig's visa renewal on the British end, his visa was expiring. Our only option to avoid separation was to marry, for me to apply for a spouse visa to the UK, to go back to Scotland with him, and to apply for his permanent residency to Canada from there. And so, with no formal proposal, I was now engaged. It has always bothered me that I never got the bended-knee, "You are my everything, marry me!" proposal that women post about on their social media with careful cropping and filters to showcase their stunning engagement rings. I didn't get my engagement ring until a year and a half after we were married! That being said, none of them got to marry Craig, so I will take my lumps with the engagement.

We were met with a reasonable amount of jeering at our decision to marry so quickly. We were accused of having a shotgun wedding. We were told we only got married for a visa. We were told it was a mistake. For some reason, Craig and me getting married because we wanted to be together seemed different to onlookers than anyone else getting married because they wanted to be together. Fortunately, neither of us has cared much about others' opinions when it comes to with whom and how we spend our love life. So, married we were, just the two of us, on June 29, 2014. In mid-October, I made the journey "hame" with Craig to Scotland.

Living in Scotland was extraordinary. The country is rustic and absolutely full of history, culture, and dare I say "wee ghosties." It is incredibly haunted if you ask me. There is something about it, an energy you can feel when you touch the walls in an ancient pub or find yourself on your own in an old corridor. My first job in Scotland was at the family-owned Galloway Arms Hotel. Mark my words, there was something in that hotel. If ever I caught myself alone, I never FELT alone. I once fibbed about hoovering the front restaurant, as when I opened the door, a heaviness swept over me, and I couldn't bring myself to step over the threshold. Upstairs, when I'd be cleaning the rooms, lights would flicker, doors would open or close, floorboards would creak, and all the while, the heaviness remained. Nothing sinister. Just a presence. I miss it now, looking back.

Our home was nestled in the Haugh of Urr, a small village with its very own pub. The Laurie Arms was my favourite place to walk to for a meal. A welcoming narrow doorway made way to a cozy bar. Upturned liquor lined the mirrored back wall, ready to be precisely measured. Hanging purposefully above the bar were the serving glasses, and above them, personal effects of the owners lined the bar wall at the dark wood ceiling. The massive stone fireplace met the wall to the right of the bar with a huge trophy fish hanging above it. Shelves built into the stones often had candles burning on them. The table next to the fireplace would one day be the place Craig and I decided together to start our family. At the end of the evening, if I listened carefully, I could hear the gentle conversations between the cows in the field next to our home as we walked up to our front door. Living in the Haugh was like a fairy tale.

Several months into my life in Scotland, one of Craig's friends was playing in a band at the Kirkpatrick Durham Village Hall, and we were invited. I was incredibly insecure in my new country, finding it difficult to cope with my anxiety. I isolated myself, only spending time with Craig and his family. I even distanced myself from workmates, concerned about who they might know and if they had ulterior motives in getting to know me. After all, everyone in every village knows everything about everyone. What must they have thought of this foreign girl Craig brought home? Some people disliked me for the simple fact that I was with Craig, and they were not. All the fears and insecurities of our courtship came flooding back anytime we were in a public setting.

Naturally, his friends would have spent time with his previous flames. I had a nagging fear that I was being compared to people in his past. I had seen myself walk into a pub on Craig's arm and groups of girls I had never met would glare at me, radiating hatred. I found the whole thing immensely intimidating. So, here I was, glancing nervously around the room of this hall, hanging onto Craig for dear life, hoping not to catch anyone staring back at me.

After the band signed off, stereo music took over and people danced, visited, and mingled for the rest of the evening. Marking the last dance, the iconic song, "Loch Lomond," rang over the speakers. As if entranced, everyone quickly gathered in the centre of the room and joined hands. Craig took my hand and told me to follow his lead. I had no idea what was happening. As I stood awkwardly in this large circle of strange people, Craig held my left hand, and a girl I didn't know took hold of my right. She linked fingers with me and smiled as if she had known me for years. As the song continued, everyone began to walk forward, slowly raising their joined hands until we had all come together at the centre, hands high in the air. Like a proud clan coming together as one. Then, as quickly as we came together, we backed away, lowering our hands as we moved back to where we started, all to the beat of the "Loch Lomond" drum. As the song gathered momentum, so too did the people in the circle. People that hadn't taken notice of each other all night were smiling and laughing together each time the circle gathered forward. By

Above all, I learned that it is absolutely possible that your soulmate can be waiting for you on the other side of the world. When you find them, your world will never be the same.

the end of the song, I couldn't help myself: I was jumping and dancing and laughing along with them, my heart absolutely racing. It brought tears to my eyes. Just like that, Scotland was home, and I never wanted to leave.

The following weekend, we arrived at the farm. Often during the weekends, we would go help, much like on that first clumsy holiday. Donald could always use a hand, especially during lambing season in the spring. We parked up, hopped on an available quad near the dog kennels, and rode up the dirt driveway about 150 metres, stone dyke to either side. We followed the road as it turned left and rode through what felt like our own forest with trees hanging over us, all the way to the top of the hill to the lambing sheds for further instruction.

It was exhilarating watching Craig in his element. I fell in love with him more each day that we lived in his home country. He was a farm boy, born and bred. I was thrilled to live that life with him. Rural

Scotland was simple, slower paced, with almost an innocence about it. I now enjoyed things like checking the sheep in each field on the back of Craig's quad, searching for fresh chicken eggs with his mother, Kaye, and walking their dozen or so dogs around the farm at night. I learned not to bother trying to collect a two-day-old lamb in the field, as you'll never catch the thing, and your jeans will end up with completely mud-stained bums if you try. I learned that a little (or a lot) of rain is actually a beautiful thing, and I welcomed the earthy smell of a Scottish downpour. It is one of the things that makes the country so breathtaking when the sun does shine. Above all, I learned that it is absolutely possible that your soulmate can be waiting for you on the other side of the world. When you find them, your world will never be the same.

I would be lying if I said it was easy to overcome the emotional turmoil that was our courtship. I am still triggered regularly by songs and memories, becoming overcome by the same anxiety, excitement, and sadness I felt those first few months. In the end, though, Craig chose me. From across the world, when he had several more convenient girls at his feet, he chose me. We have spent years after our complicated beginnings working harder than anyone I know to stay together. I spent hours toiling over the mountains of tear-stained paperwork that was required to apply for my British visa, his permanent residency to Canada, my daughter's Canadian citizenship documents, and so much more, wondering why our life had to be so difficult. I still catch myself wondering if it is all too good to be true and looking for the catch. Still, I am so grateful and proud of what we have. Together we have two beautiful children and an international love story that not many other people can boast about. When I look at our beautiful family, despite all we have been through, I can't help but feel a little bit smug.

Imagine if I had listened to all those people who thought we were crazy. Imagine if I had listened to myself on that plane ride home when I started to agree with them. Imagine if I had listened to myself when I thought this beautiful Scottish man was too good for me. All too often we are influenced by others and even by our own inner self-consciousness when things get a little tricky or seem out of reach. I encourage you to follow your heart completely, even if it takes you across the world. Imagine what your life could be.

In the words of Craig, "What's for you will not go by you."

This chapter is dedicated to Mama and Papa (Diane and Garth Turner). I would not have the life I do today if the two of you had not seen and encouraged the connection between Craig and me. My husband. My adventures in Scotland. My children. My world. I owe everything I have to you.

K.A. Henderson is the wife of a Scottish expat and a mother of two. Born and raised in the beautiful Okanagan Valley in British Columbia, she is incredibly proud of where she came from.

As a work-from-home mum with a husband who works out of town, her life is chaotic. It generally includes juggling school runs, baby naps, meal prep, endless housekeeping, a dash of writing, and above all else, self-care. Just call her the chaos coordinator!

She thought she would remain in her hometown of Kelowna all her life, as most of her family has, until she met her husband. She has since lived in Alberta, as well as southwest Scotland. She gave birth to their daughter while in Scotland before returning with her husband to the Okanagan. Four years later, she gave birth to their son. They still live in the Okanagan today, although "hame" is always on their minds.

She is well travelled, kind, and enthusiastic. She loves passionately, laughs often (mostly at herself), and worries relentlessly. Being a Libra, she has an innate desire to seek fairness and justice. This can be more trouble than it is worth to some, but to her, it is impulsive. She has a strong belief that everything happens for a reason, and she believes in all things spiritual and supernatural. Trusting life has very real meaning to her. She is thrilled to share her experiences and her imagination with the world. This is only the beginning.

Chapter Two

Birth of a Phoenix

Cayman Ferguson

The world breaks everyone, and afterward, some are strong at the broken places.

– Ernest Hemingway, A Farewell to Arms

Whether we like it or not, being a human only has a few guarantees: living, loving, hurting, and dying. The heavy certainties of life are often entangled with the delicate nature of our humanness. We live within a spectrum of positive and negative experiences, experiences that shape who we become. These experiences influence our identities; they have the ability to freeze us in time, weaken our strongest of attributes, or motivate us to become better. Sometimes it's predictable; an abundance of negative experiences will have a negative impact. Those who face the most adversity get stuck in the generational cycle of hardships. Growing up in poverty is often a predictor of poverty in adulthood. Witnessing domestic violence as a child contributes to the tolerance of it in adult relationships. Other times, resilience prevails. The struggles of our past can become the strengths of our future. Our stories get rewritten. Mine did.

In the deepest of bottoms, I knew I owed myself my future—not my past. I found motivation in connection. Finding people with whom I could relate made me feel less alone. Knowing that my rock bottom wasn't a place that I was buried in, by myself, gave me hope that I could make it out. Seeing that it was possible for me to write the end of my story, free from so much pain, encouraged me to live in a way that supported that outcome. I hope what propelled me can be found here in these words.

I was forced to learn things at an early age. Many people start life with things I didn't have, things like security, safety, and a loving home. The lack of these necessities created something inside me that most others don't get familiar with until much later: intuition, strength, and resilience. A detriment and a gift. My gift. This gift that was created out of experiencing these situations from the get-go would stick with me and carry me throughout my life. It would push me to make decisions beyond my years. It would fuel my determination to endure heartbreaks that even some adults don't have the strength to overcome. My misfortunes would ultimately serve in my journey as lessons and perspectives. It would enable me to empathize with a variety of human conditions. My love for people of all kinds was born out of relating to their darkness. These social connections have become a foundation for who I am and how I want to exist while I am here.

The difference between me and those around me was the lives we were born into. Whether it is by chance or fate, we all enter this world into a life that is already well into existence. The messy, raw reality of being alive is presented to us when we take our first breaths. The love and beauty of it all is often there to welcome us earthside and whisk us away into the naivety of childhood. But some lives lack that blissful beginning.

I was born into one unstable relationship. Two people battling their own mental health struggles. As soon as I came home, the chaos began. It would thrust me into a lifetime of hypervigilance. It would create a trauma response I've spent years unravelling. It would also rip my heart wide open to feel so much of the world in such a profound way, an intense empathy. It would create so many pieces of my identity, the strength, the people pleaser, the protector, all serving a different purpose in my survival.

Knowing that my rock bottom wasn't a place that I was buried in, by myself, gave me hope that I could make it out

My parents' relationship was not strengthened with the birth of their children; instead, it highlighted the weaknesses. My dad's addictions pulled him away from fatherhood, while my mom wanted to provide for us. She did the best she could but being a single mother of a toddler and a baby is extremely demanding, even on the strongest individuals. Inconceivable for a woman with years of suppressed trauma and mental illness. The direction our childhoods would go from so early on was, in a way, at mercy to her despair. We couldn't thrive without her guiding us. A familiar story unfolded. The story of a damaged woman who has been taught that only a man could save her. The narrative that says a woman's worth is based solely on the attention of a man. The expectation of a woman to look pretty and be subservient to the man she *belongs* to. Any man is better than no man. She gave herself to the first man that came along. And what did he give us? Fear, anxieties, and confusion. It's not only what our family gained because of him, it's also what we lost: innocence, harmony, and trust. I found ways to protect myself and those around me. I grew up far earlier than I should have. I became strong.

When we find ourselves at that fork in the road, one path prolonging our pain and the other catapulting us forward, it likely won't be a clear-cut journey. First, we typically run to safety and comfort. The things that make us feel safe initially aren't always the healthiest. When you're sad and reach for the ice cream, or you get pissed off and need a drink, it goes to show how we seek instant gratification. I've been anorexic, soothing my neglect with starvation and praise from others. I've been the anxious girl, smoking a joint to numb out. I've recklessly turned to drinking and drugs to feel anything at all. I binged countless times after pushing my perfectionism to its breaking point. I spent so long angry at myself for choosing the coping methods I did. The shame and guilt surrounding every unhealthy choice I was making made me hate myself. How can we be mad at our brains for trying to survive? We are so hardwired to think these survival techniques are bad that we somehow turn to them out of laziness. We are taught that this form of self-preservation is useless and destructive. The reality? We're all just trying to get through each moment the best we can. Once we start to be gentle on ourselves and practice self-forgiveness, we can empathize with the part of us that is hurting. We can hold space for that part of us, and we can choose to take steps toward a better path. The poor coping skills we first chose can serve their purpose. They can be part of the strength in our own story if we let them. We can use those methods to carry us to the moments that require all the courage and bravery to pivot. There are so many ways we can transform one situation. When we take responsibility for improving our situation, that is when our power can thrive.

The birth of your inner Phoenix begins.

9-1-1

By the age of eight, I was skilled at keeping my home life secret. I was old enough to feel ashamed about what went on behind closed doors, yet young enough that I didn't understand that it wasn't due to any fault of mine. The alcoholism, domestic violence, and neglect had nothing to do with me. It felt like some wound I carried around that wouldn't heal. I carried the burden of it all. If I let it show, it would reveal my weakness. The weakness of my parents became the scars I was desperate to keep hidden. I thought I hid them so well.

Not only was I good at telling people what they wanted to hear, I also became incredibly intuitive, a necessity from growing up in my home. I distinctly remember entering the kitchen from the staircase while my mom made coffee every morning, and I'd be able to read her. I'd know if the night would bring violence. All the intricate movements, the tone of voice—I could predict the future. It allowed me to prepare for what would come. I'd make my safety plan. As a child that saw my life as shameful, asking for help did not come easily; it didn't really come at all. I'd managed to figure things out while sparing myself the pity of others. But just as things often do in life, everything changed in an instant.

It was a regular evening. My parents were drunk and arguing. My stepbrother was in his room. I was watching TV with the volume low enough to keep tabs on the fight happening downstairs. I'd periodically go down to feel the tension in the room. If things were simmering down, a weight would lift, and I could go and enjoy cartoons before bed. If things were escalating, I knew just how to use myself. I could talk to my mom, try and reason with her and encourage her to leave it alone. If you've ever tried reasoning with an intoxicated and emotional adult, it's quite the feat. It is much harder when you're a kid.

"Mom, I know he's a jerk."

"Yes, Mom, I know you're right."

You have to earn their trust. You must be on their side to sway them.

These are the types of things I'd figured out while my friends were figuring out how to tie their shoes. If I couldn't calm one parent down, I'd have to try the other.

"My mom is just drunk, she doesn't mean what she is saying."

"Please, I know she's just upset and being mean."

More often than not, their argument would end uneventfully, but a few times a month, that wasn't the case. Those nights would get loud, messy, and sometimes physical. The following morning would always bring sobriety, even if it was short-lived.

This night in particular would completely alter our reality. The way their argument escalated, I knew this night wasn't going to end well. I crouched myself in the hallway to be close enough to intervene in a second, if needed. I watched as my mom and stepdad threw insults back and forth until hands got involved. I tried physically throwing myself in, but the rage had set in. Anger blinded them. As I was shoved to the side, I watched a hand around my mom's neck steal her voice, and soon, her breath. Her face started turning a shade of purple, and I knew my secret wasn't protecting me anymore. I ran to the phone and dialled 9-1-1. I didn't just ask for help, I begged for it. I recognized that this was bigger than me. I knew that our reputation wasn't worth risking a life over. The police came, and while it saved my mom's life, it also resulted in numerous foster homes and my parents losing custody.

That's the potential of reaching out when you're drowning. The rescue boat might not be on the most enjoyable waters, but it will do its job. You have to know when to surrender, or your pride can be fatal.

Ultimatum

Life with addicted parents makes for extremely difficult teenage years. The angst and the rebellion are a lot less appealing when you have no one protesting them. Stay out all weekend? No big deal. Get drunk? That's fine, they are too.

I can't say from experience but from typical stories of challenging teenage years, it's the parents pleading with the kids to make better choices. The parents are the ones throwing out ultimatums to resolve their youth's behaviours. In my house it was the opposite. After being reunited with my mom at ten years old after over a year in the social services system, I thought things would be different. I had spent so much time while I was away dreaming of how much my mom would have changed to become the mom I always wanted her to be. I was wrong. Not much had changed. Same parents, same addictions, same unresolved issues. So, when things slowly started to look more and more like our life before I entered foster care, I can't say I was surprised. As I got older, I found my own ways to escape.

I was twelve the first time I smoked marijuana. Shortly after, I began drinking alcohol, regularly blacking out and getting sick. I would use food to fill a void. It all had a thrill to it for a short time. My friends started getting caught, and their parents would punish them. Then, it became lonely. I'd tell myself I was lucky to have parents who didn't care. In reality, my friends' consequences opened me to the lack of attention I got. I craved what they had. I wanted a reaction. I wanted someone to care enough to put my best interest first and to give me tough love. It never came.

My partying was short-lived. It only highlighted what I wasn't getting. I sunk into a depression I'd never previously experienced. I was desperate for attention. I felt so alone and angry at my parents. Nothing seemed more important than their drinking. I could feel myself slipping lower and lower. If home was causing my pain, then leaving it had to be my solution. So that's what I did at fourteen years old, a terrible conclusion to come to as a child. I wanted better. I knew I owed it to myself to make sure I could be in an environment that would support my growth. Leaving was one of the most heartbreaking things I could do. My mom and I were so intertwined through all the trauma we'd endured together and choosing to leave her felt so wrong. She was supposed to be the one making the tough choices, not me. I'd asked for so many years for her not to drink. I'd been taken away from her because of her drinking. She couldn't manage to get sober. It was no longer my responsibility to stay.

So, I left with the ultimatum that if she could quit drinking, I would return. An ultimatum that went unanswered, proof that I wasn't worth fighting for. If no one was going to fight *for* me, it would be up to me.

For Myself

As I matured and became more cognizant of the instability in my life, I was still unaware of how deep the effects of it were. I would joke with friends that despite it all, I was totally fine. When I was relying on unhealthy coping mechanisms, I was oblivious to what was truly going on. The substance use, food, distraction—anything to avoid my emotions—were my protective shields for how intensely I was suffering. I slowly started hating who I was. I hated my home life. I hated that I was poor. I hated my parents' addictions. I hated my body. I wanted any escape I could get.

When I left home at fourteen, I ended up at my stepsister's house. She was grown and had a family of her own. As my dad and stepmom's drug addiction spiralled out of control and my mom and stepdad's alcoholism took over, she took in my brother and me. She was thirty-one and had her sixteen and fourteen-year-old siblings living with her, along with her own two children.

When I joined her household at the end of grade nine, she was recently postpartum and trying to lose some baby weight by following Weight Watchers. I was so insecure with my body and appearance that it seemed like the perfect thing to work on over the summer before I started at a new school in a new city. My perfectionist tendencies grabbed hold of the weight loss and what started as an innocent diet plummeted into anorexia. I spent a whole school year shrinking myself with the belief I was being "healthy." I had been neglected for so long that the attention I received from changing my body felt like a drug I couldn't get enough of.

The hunger gave me a high. The pain in my stomach was a confirmation that I was succeeding at my goal. The praise from the people around me fuelled my fire. I felt like I had transformed from the old version of me I loathed so much into a more desirable version. It did not occur to me that my obsession was anything but healthy. I found it so easy to tell myself I had just created a new lifestyle when I was over-exercising, restricting, and starving to death. Toward the end of the school year, rumours started circulating that I had an eating disorder. Me, an eating disorder? No way. I was in control. I was controlling everything I consumed and how much I moved. That was dedication, not an illness. I believed this until I binged for the first time.

A natural consequence of prolonged restriction is bingeing. After about a year of intense restriction, I had an episode that was so unfamiliar to me. I started eating, and I couldn't stop. I ate until I was sick. My abdomen was physically distended and painful. Even more than my physical pain, I felt like the biggest failure. I blamed myself for being so weak. I was so mad that I could undo all the progress I'd made. What kind of disgusting human can't stop eating? My lack of understanding about what was happening made me feel so ashamed. I promised myself it would never happen again.

Bingeing isn't a matter of willpower, it is your innate survival skills. It wasn't my weakness, it was my most primitive form of perseverance. Binges were infrequent in the beginning. It was easy to dismiss until the intervals between binges got shorter. Once a month, once a week, days in a row. If you've ever experienced a binge-eating episode, then you know the worst part is the immense amount of guilt, shame, and self-loathing that comes afterward. When it became frequent, I knew there was something wrong. My google searches came up with the same results: Eating Disorders. I felt so damaged. For so long it was other people's battles I was trying to fight, how could I be the one that needed saving?

I walked into the high school counsellor's office one morning and confessed that I needed help. No parents, no guardian advocating for me. I was on my own. That first time I reached out would be what led to my outpatient treatment, hospitalizations, and months of inpatient treatment. I ended up being treated in an inpatient program twice during my grade twelve year. The first time, I'd failed miserably upon discharge. When I was in the program, I watched the other kids' families come together to nurture and encourage them. Their families were part of their solution. I had no one. I allowed myself to pick up old behaviours while feeling sorry for myself. I was wishing I had someone to unload some of the responsibility on.

Days into my second hospitalization, one of the nurses that I'd grown close with gave it to me straight:

"Cayman, you can't expect that someone is going to save you. The other kids have something that you don't and that is just the way it is. If you want to beat this, it's going to be up to you."

As much as those words stung, it was the hard truth I needed to hear. It had to be me. I had to make it work. Twelve years later and I've navigated my way, solo, through recovery and my mental health. I spend more days winning than struggling. I am so proud that I've fought to be where I am now, as a woman and mother.

From the Ashes

I was twenty-four when my daughter was born. During the years I was learning to live with the traumas I'd experienced, she was a gift. It took time to become conscious of my past without letting it consume me. She was the most beautiful reminder of why I had spent my life pushing for more. I found myself in a position I never truly believed I would be in. I was married to a wonderful man. It was safe for me to be open and honest about my mental illness. My husband and I purchased our first home. I was achieving all of what my brain had convinced me I was unworthy of.

In the years leading up to my pregnancy, I'd dealt with some frequent medical issues. Because I was still integrating the traumas I'd lived through, it seemed more likely that these ailments were physical manifestations of my mental health. This was validated by most of the medical professionals I found myself in front of. Even after some real diagnoses, there was still no title for what I found myself living with. When my daughter was ten months old, I hit a wall. My body couldn't continue.

I questioned myself for months. I was convinced that I was somehow causing this. The same guilt from my childhood returned—it must be *my* fault. I had all the excuses: stress, fatigue, parenthood. I felt that I was slipping away. The person and mom I wanted to be was out of reach due to the limitations of my body. It was a process, but I finally got an answer: late-stage neurological Lyme disease. The diagnosis felt like just as much a mystery as when I was seeking answers.

So many questions and concerns suffocated me. There are many conflicting opinions on the disease and its treatment. The financial burden can be huge. We were a young, single-income family. Everything I had worked so hard for seemed like it could unravel so easily. I almost let myself drown in self-doubt; I didn't know if I had more fight in me. It wasn't fair. A few months into my treatment, I found out I was pregnant with my son. Instead of the pregnancy bringing joy and excitement, it was met with fear and worry. I allowed myself to sit in the negativity briefly, then my perspective changed. This could be another reminder that I could rise above.

After a healthy pregnancy, my son was born, and my Lyme disease returned. I tried to juggle my wellness while learning how to be a mom of two. After years of putting everyone else first, I knew, now more than ever, I had to come first. It felt so counterintuitive, me over my babies. I'd never been good at being selfish, but putting my treatment first wasn't for me—it would mean I could be there for my kids. In fall of 2018, when my son was six months old and my daughter was under three, I boarded a plane alone. I left for two weeks to undergo stem cell treatment. Many of the insecurities I had throughout the years resurfaced. As I sat with myself during my time away, it was all too familiar. I was fighting *for* myself yet again. I had all those experiences from my past to create an even bigger fire inside. A fire I would use to complete an intensive medical procedure and jump back into motherhood.

When I returned home from my treatment, it was supposed to be a time of healing. But again, I found myself navigating heartbreak. One of my best friends unexpectedly passed away. She was a woman I had grown alongside for more than a decade. We first bonded as teenagers, and we birthed our children within weeks of one another. She was a beautiful soul, and processing the unexplainable loss drained me. My physical healing became overshadowed by my emotional healing. I knew I couldn't allow myself to become weak in her departure. I had to stoke my fire. This had to be a log I could add to build my internal fire even bigger, in her honour. I used my grief to step into my power. I was choosing to end 2019 being powerful.

Power is what I'd need—what the whole world would need—in the year to come. The pandemic. That word alone still has the ability to evoke the uncertainty we all felt in the early days. The world shut down. My powerful self crumbled under the unprecedented pressures of this new reality. My OCD spun out of control to the deepest I'd ever fallen. I could barely get through each day. The husband I never dreamed of having was there to be the man I'd never known existed. Together, we found my way out. I was being loved. I was being helped. After a lifetime of feeling so lonely in the pursuit of living, I realized I'd achieved the dream life I had envisioned as a child.

The pandemic shook me hard, but what it woke me up to was myself. I'd spent so many years expanding who I was, in so many directions, that I forgot to nurture my core. I forgot the basics. I forgot that fire cannot burn without oxygen. I forgot to take care of myself. I began seeing a trauma-specialized therapist, exercising regularly, and fuelling my soul with all the nourishment I could get. I started my mission to fill my life with intentional things. Things that rejuvenate me: friendships, hobbies, pleasure. Each day that passes adds its own form of kindling to the fire that has been burning for the past thirty years. I continue to stoke this fire. I am so proud to stand back and admire the flames I've created. How I've managed to become who I am from the ashes. A Phoenix.

The world breaks everyone, but I refuse to be broken.

Lucas, for always believing I can. Maeva & Kesler, for transforming my experience as a woman.

Cayman Ferguson is a woman dedicated to connection. She is a full-time mama, living in the beautiful Okanagan with her husband, daughter, son, and dog. Cayman's journey has enabled her to develop a deep empathy for a variety of challenges that many face in their own lives. By navigating her own trauma, she became inspired to show up for other women. Whether it's enjoying a good cup of coffee, getting outside to move her body, or sipping a glass of red in the evening, Cayman is always looking to approach everything with mindfulness and gratitude. The kitchen is where she escapes and expresses her creativity in her spare time. Cayman believes in triumphing over any obstacles thrown in her path, and she hopes to help others believe that too.

Chapter Three

Ignite, It's an Inside Job

Sharlet Mentes

I would love to bring you into the kitchen of my home. I have to say that the overall thread throughout my life has had many beautiful and painful moments that for some reason took place in my kitchen. This central hub of life.

I married young and had not fully grown or developed into who I was at the core. Life happens fast and somewhere between saying "I do," buying a house, and having three kids, I lost who I was and was left navigating these uncharted waters feeling alone.

To my surprise, the most alone I ever felt was sitting next to someone. I didn't feel seen, supported, or cherished. Alone because health issues left me as the main supporter, planning, coordinating, and raising three little humans. You don't lose yourself instantly, it's a long, slow, drawn-out process where you turn away from your truth and settle for little things each day, which, in turn, makes you feel small.

You don't start out promising forever, believing it will be anything short of that.

One day the scales tipped, and I felt more afraid of staying stuck than I did about facing up to the conversation I needed to have. We could no longer stay together the way things were. Late one evening I found myself in the kitchen with my husband at the time. I was lacking the ability to recognize and communicate my feelings for the most part, but I knew one thing for sure: "I don't want to settle for mediocre!" I said. I was always a dreamer and had ended up at a place in my life where I had lost my fire inside; my flame was dim and flickering. I was NUMB. So many things brought me to this realization.

It was almost like an out-of-body experience. I had played it in my head but then it just spilled out, raw and unfiltered. I was both observing the interaction from afar while feeling a swarm of numbing emotions that took my breath away and made me cringe. Even my nervous laugh came out. I mean, what is the appropriate response one should have? These moments are bigger than we can process; this trauma creates a response and we react, tipping us into fight-or-flight mode.

That day, like icy winds, hit me in the face, my lips chapped, brows furrowed. This was too big a storm to ride out. This ship was going down, splitting stem to stern and flooding with oceans between us. The process was very fluid and unpredictable, a swell of feelings that rose and fell out of sync with each other. Yet in the middle of all these feelings, we, as parents, still needed to provide stability for our little ones when our worlds fell apart.

I think the worst part of it all wasn't losing him, it was losing me.

"Insanity is doing the same thing over and over again and expecting different results."

–Albert Einstein

I began to realize that I had to take back control of how I allowed others to treat me. At first, I put up small boundaries, but this grew to ignite the HOPE in creating a life I loved once more.

Keeping this part of my life separate from the person I have become seemed the right thing to do, until now. In reflection, I realize it was the raw connection and wisdom from those who had gone before that gave me hope. If they could do it, I would be able to! What I needed was someone to tell me that the light at the end of the tunnel wasn't a train! I couldn't see a light, and if I imagined one, it seemed like it would only end in tragedy.

Perspective: What if we got to a place in our lives where our level of awareness and growth allowed us to heal and not repeat the hurt? What a gift it would be to our children and to future generations to be able to see where we are reactive and to learn ways to take a deep breath and consciously choose our actions. Learning to practice non-judgment allows us to hold space to choose kindness.

What you think, you create.

What you feel, you attract.

What you imagine, you become.

I remember that through all my transitions—school, job change, becoming a parent, separation and divorce—I had these stand-out moments when people said a sentence or two that resonated so deeply it hit a nerve, awakening something deep, something that I didn't want to turn off. This awakening helped me see things clearly and notice where I was giving up small pieces of myself by coasting unconsciously through my pain.

Not long after the kitchen awakening, I walked into my place of work and a coworker said, "Are you okay? I don't see that light in your eyes, that spark. I'm worried about you." I knew what they were talking about. I was a shell of a person, so afraid of the reactions of those close to me. I spent most of my time trying to please my children and make others happy. I felt stuck; my free spirit was so weighed down that I felt I was ready to GIVE UP. It felt too daunting of a task to stand up to fight against this feeling of being trapped. Settling when I was so tired seemed so much easier.

It often seems shocking or surprising that behind our "white picket fences," which appear so good on the outside, we forget that sometimes we are staying silent inside, turning away from each other and building walls. Maybe we should remind ourselves that no one truly knows what happens behind closed doors and that there are always two sides to every story. What we are specifically responsible for is challenging our assumptions and being honest with ourselves. When I started rebuilding, I wanted to make sure that my foundation was built on my own two feet. I had learned to use a crutch of relying on the tripod of codependency, but when one leg gets pulled out, you lose balance because you are no longer familiar with how to stand on two feet. You have to relearn balance, and just like training muscles, you have to retrain your mind to believe you can support yourself.

I think one of the most detrimental things is ISOLATION, and this type of control leaves you feeling and believing you are alone, stuck inside your head, playing words over and over again that you are not worthy, not enough, and broken. Isolation fuels bitterness, resentment, and anger. Your surroundings really can make you sick: stress is still one of the number one causes of illness and disease. I was in DENIAL that what my partner and I had was not respectful or healthy. I needed to take action, but the fear of speaking up was holding me back.

I was WORRIED about how the choices in my life would affect my children. As a mama, I think the most powerful thing for me was to feel that I had tried everything I could. So when in my heart of hearts I truly believed it was better for my children and me to leave than to stay, I was able to move forward unwaveringly. I believed that ripping off the bandage so to speak, was a much kinder approach with separation than some of the "back-and-forths" I had observed.

"Our suffering comes from our attachment to people and things, our repeated attempts to find something lasting where there is nothing lasting to be found."

–Philip Martin, The Zen Path Through Depression

I felt like I was falling while trying to build my wings on the way down, not willing to fully let go. I was holding on for dear life when inches below my feet was new territory that was just waiting for me to discover it. Weeks into living on my own for the first time in my life, the panic attacks started or, as my sweet daughter calls them, "mini heart attacks of fear." Heartbreakingly true. I couldn't breathe; this was a new intense and unfamiliar space. It took many more attacks until I started to take action, taking back control of the power I had given up.

Facing one daunting task at a time, I started pulling myself forward out of the muck. If someone wasn't respecting my boundaries and was incapable of treating me the way I deserved, then I was ENABLING that behaviour by staying and allowing someone to treat me poorly. In other words, we need to know when to walk away! This was not what I wanted to hear from the counsellor; I wanted someone who sided with me and allowed me to wallow in the pain of where I was at.

I had an amazing financial adviser, and his words were worth as much to me as the counsellor's. I remember him telling me, "You have the power, take back control!" To this day it was one of the most powerful mental shifts that I had to make, and it filtered down into every area of my life.

My brother's support, once I made my decision to separate, was incredible. He met me every week and we worked out together and then went back to his place and made some incredibly delicious and power-packed recovery food. Words just flow easier in the kitchen as you methodically go through the steps of preparing recipes you know by heart. He EMPOWERED me to see my potential when I was at my rock bottom. He had my back, he stood up for me, and he even took the time in his bachelor pad to blow up an air mattress and get a pillow and blanket ready for me whenever I needed to collapse. He was a safe place for my heavy heart to rest.

My brother is the same person who said five years later with his face beaming how he wished I could see just how far I'd grown and that he is so proud of me. He asked if I wanted his opinion of my new partner at the time and I said to him, "You know what, this is right for me." I had succeeded in feeling confident enough not to need others' approval.

When I looked in the mirror over the last couple years before I separated, the person I saw in the reflection was gripped by the overwhelming intensity of the circumstances. I barely laughed, and I had migraines and tension headaches all the time. I felt the tops of my eyelids darken from the glooming depression that lingered day in and day out. When I looked in the rearview mirror and saw the kids looking at me with eyes that wanted nothing more than to see me happy again, it gave me goosebumps. I couldn't change others or make them happy, but I could be responsible for my own happiness! It's an inside job. Change sheds the old and gives birth to the new.

Let's just be real here: no two people are the same, so don't let anyone tell you what's right for you! Divorce is not ideal, and there just isn't a specific formula. Even being amicable doesn't mean it is without pain and suffering. Change is hard. Transitions force you to face unfamiliar and unpredictable obstacles. Adjusting and readjusting on the fly. I was juggling so many things. I definitely dropped some balls along the way. I learned that most of the time you can just pick them back up and try again. Becoming more comfortable with uncertainty began opening up new possibilities in life.

For me, I needed the time and space to see things clearly. The analogy I like to use is treading water in a muddy pond—you need time and space to let the water settle, so you can see things more clearly. When you are fighting so hard to just stay afloat, you don't have the perspective or the clarity to have any chance of moving forward.

Setting up new boundaries in one relationship spilled over into all my relationships. I realized ways in which I could improve my communication and put up boundaries. I had to find the power to face what I feared the most: loneliness, unworthiness, judgment, and guilt. I found it a little bit easier each time I started to fight for me. I began to change the negative connotation of the word SELFISH that is sometimes implied, realizing it is actually incorrect with regard to oneself. This change made me braver to ask for what I wanted and fight for it fiercely. This step of faith fuelled my fire!

As a healthcare worker in geriatrics, I often deal with people who have had up to a century of wisdom. There are two main types of people: those who stay raw, real, and open, and those who are hardened, bitter, and resentful about what life has to offer. How can two people who go through relatively similar and traumatic experiences come out completely different? From my observation and clinical experience, it really comes down to mindset. We are always in control of what we do with our thoughts, if nothing else.

IT'S OKAY TO MAKE MISTAKES! THAT'S HOW YOU LEARN!

The signing of the separation agreement and sale of our family home was the epicentre of the storm that landed me in the hospital for a week due to the cumulative stress. After being discharged home, I decided to go on a three-day silent retreat to give my body a chance to restart and recover. There, I learned about different types of mediation. All I had known about it until then was sitting on the floor, and to be honest, it sounded ridiculous when I thought of all the things that I needed to do while working full-time and raising three kids! I realized that meditation was, in fact, a mindset not a physical position. I found ways that worked for me: walking meditation, meditating while washing the dishes after the kids go to bed, running, hiking, and listening to music. I started to nurture a sense of CALM in the chaos.

I found JOY at the same time as I had PAIN. I became more aware of my feelings, realizing it is common to feel many conflicting and contrasting emotions at the same time.

How true it is that we listen to music when we're happy but it's the lyrics that really touch our souls when we're struggling. Music shaped my healing path. Music gave me power and perspective and let me feel, heal, and make sense of the journey. I created a powerful playlist that fuelled and harnessed my fire! Music that helped me get back up, dust off, and try again. I fought to keep myself raw and open. In between the cracks the light shines through if only we keep our hearts open. "Sun Is Shining" by Axwell Ingrosso featuring Kygo was one of the first songs that twinged this inside me along with "Fight Song" by Rachel Platten.

Exercise gave me a positive outlet when things got so intense that it felt like I got sucker-punched in the face. I remember running until I felt like I could breathe again. There are so many forms of physical exercise that can work, but it was running that worked for me and eased this pain and helped me avoid numbing myself.

For the first time in a decade, it felt like I had "alone time." I had time again, but I seemed unable to sit with my feelings of heartbreak and was too exhausted to just enjoy it. In these baby steps forward, I started what has now turned into a tradition I call "ice cream moments." When I sat down in the kitchen one day to reflect and try and figure out who I was again, the ONLY thing I knew for sure in the entire world I felt like having was tiger ice cream. Tiger ice cream is deeply rooted in our family lineage, and I find joy in the connection and closeness it brings to me. Oftentimes I have tea in the spirit of someone close to me who is separated by miles. I sit in my kitchen and feel them nearby. Going through the steps of a family recipe felt reassuring, connecting generation to generation. This feeling of connection to someone I look up to and love deeply warms my heart.

During this time, I remember a packed lunch that stood out with its blaring sirens of alarm. I had cold veggie hotdogs still in their package (cold because I couldn't care less), and I grabbed a couple ketchup and mustard packets from the cafeteria and plunked down at the lunch table. I remember a coworker who couldn't help but comment on how horrifying my lunch was! It makes me laugh now when I imagine it years later. I had to learn to fill my cup first. That fall, I took a day off around my birthday just for me to pursue the sensory experience of going to the farmers' market. I took time to smell, touch, and taste. I came home unrushed and made a beautiful dish of hand-picked mushrooms fried with homemade pasta, sauce, and some delicious fresh herbs. I sat alone and learned to infuse more joy and simple pleasures into my life.

Perspective: If divorce is an adult problem, then let's grow up and find ways to ease the suffering and not make our kids pay for it! Although we may strive for this, with tears in our eyes we comfort our little ones when words lack the glue to keep their hearts from breaking. It is hard; it is an unideal situation. We try to minimize this suffering with creativity and innovation. We can always do better and learn more. Let's change, so future generations can benefit from our progressiveness.

Trust your gut and let it guide you as my Nagymama, my Hungarian grandma, always says. What a gift to be able to recognize the positive qualities in another woman and to help build them up. I appreciate the people who made an effort to do this, creating a healthier and more supportive community.

I printed out all the stages of grief as I began to find myself shifting back and forth through emotions. This allowed me to recognize and understand people's reactions as well as my own. The opposite of depression is expression. I remember mid-week after a long workday, grabbing a bottle of wine and collapsing onto my kitchen floor in my single-wide trailer, tears streaming down my face. The weight of the grief and intense feeling of loss I was experiencing were crushing. Humans need a certain amount of consistency and predictability to thrive. Intense times of transition cause increased turmoil as things become unfamiliar and unpredictable.

Right around this time I was connected to the work of Brené Brown. My soul was thirsty to learn what I could have done differently. I cared about what others said, and their words grated my soul—a soul that was inhabiting the shell of the person I had become. It was pivotal for me to learn to let go of other people's judgments. This is one of the quotes that helped me realize not everyone's criticism counts. It helped me to start the journey toward inner peace and forgiving myself.

In her book *Daring Greatly*, Brené Brown harkened back to a speech that Teddy Roosevelt gave in 1910. Roosevelt said:

> "It is not the critic who counts; not the man who points out how the strong man stumbles, or where the doer of deeds could have done them better. The credit belongs to the man who is actually in the arena, whose face is marred by dust sweat and blood; who strives valiantly; who errs, who comes short again and again, because there is no effort without error and shortcoming; but who does actually strive to do the deeds; who knows great enthusiasms, the great deviations; who spends himself in a worthy cause; who at the best knows

in the end the triumph of high achievement, and who at the worst, if he fails, at least fails while daring greatly."

Moving forward, I preserved more of my precious energy to fight for what was most important. Picking my battles, just like parenting. Letting go of some of the fights gave me the freedom from the control of others.

Perspective: Find what is important in your heart and fight for that.

I needed more help, more physical touch, more connection, less turning away, more fighting for me, and more help in raising three young children. It still makes me glow when I think that I have found that. You really do attract others. Do the work on the inside; trust me, it's worth it!

Sitting on the couch five years later, being offered a glass of water and insisting I sit and let them get it. In this moment I realized I don't have to be the giver, the one to jump up and serve others as conditioned by society. This time I am accepting help and allowing myself to rejuvenate in the joy that comes from finally learning to not do it all and feeling supported in that. As I sit here writing, I can hear my partner mixing up an exquisite meal prepared by the hands of someone who loves me the same way I have always loved.

"Our job is not to deny the story, but to defy the ending — to rise strong, recognize our story, and rumble with the truth until we get to a place where we think, yes. This is what happened. And I will choose how the story ends."

–Brené Brown, Rising Strong

As I sit here, rain falling on my tent in the clean, crisp air and the quiet of nature all around, its stillness is refreshing my soul. This time spent in nature reiterates that the best views truly do come after the hardest climbs. She wakes with a fire in her eyes recharged by the moon, the stars, and a blissful sleep—a sleep she is newly getting used to that comes from aligned values and truths that create an environment that is suitable for growth. My body is responding very well to my mind.

The energy that connects all living things: plants, trees, humans. If we resist the call of what wakes us up inside, we stay dormant. All living organisms are like leaves on the same tree of life!

Trees best describe growth, their roots being grounded, their branches bursting with desire to change and grow. It's an inside job—all the work on the inside starts to show with new growth. Like rings on a tree trunk, it is important to remember that the tough years give us the most strength. Some years have few while others burst forth with lush and expansive new growth. I call on the natural law of attraction for

We are always stronger than we know and just a glimmer of hope is all we need to see a way through.

more abundance and ease as I go through my life, and I wish the same for you.

Wise women pause between the years to honour what is in each of us. The sharing of this wisdom can be extremely helpful in making sense of where you're at and in sifting through the barrage of opinions and judgments that will come your way. As you sit down and pick up this book, you connect to this frequency of women. Helping you rekindle the fire that's inside you! Yes, you, you beautiful and amazing human!

I wish for you soon to see the first crack of light at the end of your tunnel—the light coming from the sun shining through the other side of this mountain you must climb. We are always stronger than we know and just a glimmer of hope is all we need to see a way through.

Develop gently and dig your roots deep into what your soul finds nourishing; use this to amplify your forward movement.

To challenge you to: find your voice again and trust your gut.

To help you to: be vulnerable and brave enough to lean into the prickly points and grow.

To not settle for: mediocre, and to live a raw, inspiring life.

To show up for: yourself and others in your life.

My challenge for you is to take one step in the direction you know you need to take. One step that fuels the fire to build a flame once again inside your soul. We only have ONE life, which evaporates if we don't pause and enjoy the present grind and ease into enjoying the things we can where we are at.

With a twinkle in my eyes and fire in my heart, I learn to find pleasure in the climb. And that has changed my view, allowing me to hold space to show up and be present in each moment.

We are more the same than we are different.

This new sense of self shines the light, illuminating, helping us see the directions that are pulling us forward. The radiance comes from our inner insight and intuition as we move along the stepping stones toward our new directions.

Burn bright, my darlin', burn bright.

Yours truly, Sharlet Mentes

This book wouldn't be in your hands if Sharlet hadn't been forged in the fires she walked through and had been challenged by the many warriors with hearts of gold.

I want to extend the warmest gratitude to my Nagymama (grandmother) who told me to trust my gut and believe in the law of attraction. Her intuitive energy is close, no matter the miles.

To my parents, Alex and Gay, who instilled in me many wonderful values and encouraged me to stay inquisitive in life.

To my husband, Tim, I'm so glad that our worlds collided and became one. You are philosophical, you have a huge heart, and you aren't afraid of a big challenge. I've found someone who hugged all my broken pieces back together. You make me feel seen and cherished.

Lastly, for the one who had my back when I needed it the most and helped me expand my mindset and empowered me to see my worth, my brother, A.J.

Where I came from: This thing called life. Sharlet Mentes arrived earthside in Calgary, Alberta. She grew up in a small town of northern British Columbia with her parents and brother. This shaped her in many ways, including creating her deep connection with nature and love for mountains and adventuring outdoors.

Lifelong growing: Sharlet has lived in Kelowna, British Columbia, for two decades now and has worked in healthcare for fifteen years. She has always been fascinated by the anatomy and function of the human body and all the cascade of processes and interconnected networks that keep us alive and well. Sharlet enjoys learning from her three beautiful children and loves watching her family grow. She raises them with her husband and their father who she is separated from, and this has challenged her to be innovative. Love multiplies, never divides.

She is a runner and has raced as far away as New Zealand. She has completed a 50 km ultra-race, marathons, half marathons, etc. Sharlet volunteers as the vice president of the local Kelowna Running Club.

Sharlet considers herself a lifelong learner and is working toward her bachelor's degree. She is a co-owner in the start-up company Momentous Coffee Co, which has been a fun build as they are turning a '78 camper van into a coffee vendor!

Sharlet is a dreamer and has big goals. Her heart will forever belong by the water and her head in the clouds. Maybe that's why she loves the mountains so much?

Chapter Four

Present Over Perfect

Marika Soleil

I lost a part of me this past year. A very important part of me that has caused me to question so much more about myself and my reality. She was not my better half by any means, but she did teach me many lessons, and for that, I salute her.

I experienced some major changes these last few months and my life will be forever altered by the circumstances I had to deal with and the decisions I made. From extreme highs to extreme lows, this year was full of them. I have had so much success in my entire life yet so much hardship, and it seems to all have come crashing down in 2021. Through it all, the fierce grit that lies inside me has gotten me through it, but I know it's not over yet, and here I am, one more chapter away from yet another new beginning.

I got to the point of not being able to keep up to myself and my unbalanced, overloaded life. I was all over the place and everywhere, all at the same time. Nothing was meaningful anymore. I was in a daily non-stop cycle of doing for the sake of doing. I slowly lost myself in the hamster wheel of busyness, and I completely forgot about myself and what mattered to me. When it was time to relax from all the stress from the day, I would cope with one of my BFFs, wine, to get through it. Stress and alcohol are two very powerful things, and when mixed together, led me into a very heavily defeated state.

I was so tired. I was so anxious. I was so angry, and so unfulfilled.

This wasn't the true me, but for years I had moulded myself into this pattern, I had created this habit. The true me was flipped full circle. Everything I liked to do was lost. From choosing to use my extra time hiking, running, and cooking, I suddenly had no hobbies. Instead, I had irrelevant tasks that I had created for myself that would cause me great stress. I went from being the most social and active friend who always planned get-togethers and dinner parties to losing the connections I had with all my friends and family, leaving me isolated in my head and in my heart. Life was on repeat for me for years. That's not enjoyable!

"Sometimes things fall apart, so better things can fall together."

–Marilyn Monroe

When I started "growing up" so many years ago, I wanted to be everything. I wanted all the things: nice things, money, an illustrious career, the perfect family, and above all, I wanted all the attention. Most importantly, I wanted everyone else to know this about me and know that I was able to accomplish all of it on my own. I needed to show everyone that I could do it and do it better than anyone else!

My subconscious was telling me that I was wrong, but I wasn't listening, and I just kept going to achieve all the things I wanted in life. Instead, while building this famed life, I was slowly shutting down. I kept adding more to my plate. It was always more, more, more, and if it wasn't more, then it was "this isn't good enough, I need more." I was drowning and deep down looking for some kind of sign, but I wouldn't accept any signs . . . no matter what happened in my life, negative or positive, it had no effect. I just kept going.

Allow me to introduce myself. My name is Marika. I have impeccable drive, and I live the fast life of an entrepreneur with an addictive personality, a sprinkle of OCD, a splash of stubbornness, a large pinch of perfectionism, and a whole lot of people-pleasing by trying to make everything right for everybody but myself. I am a working mom who feels like I have to prove myself. I love my friend, wine, even when I know she's trouble for me, and I am the queen of problem-solving everyone else's problems while adding to my own.

Welcome to my story.

I came into 2021 starting the year with one of the most successful years of my real estate career, sixteen years in the making. Such hard work was finally beginning to come together. New business plan. New team. New office. New outlook, and an enormous amount of business coming in from all the groundwork I had put in. I was on schedule to do a massive number of transactions this year, until everything came to a screeching halt in the spring.

It came to a halt because of my weaknesses that I never accounted for in a negative way. The lack of letting things go, wanting to be everything at once, my perfectionism, and people-pleasing that led me down a dark spiral to the chapter of life I call "chronic stress and burnout phase." Mix stress with terrible coping mechanisms like alcohol and isolation plus a pandemic, and you've got a very tricky situation.

All the things I thought were good about me were actually bad, and they cost me. They cost me the deterioration of my mental and physical health. What was next?

I believe everyone is in some way suffering silently because they just don't have all the answers. None of us do, and there is nothing that can change that. What can change is your mindset, your habits, and your being in a way that is okay with not knowing everything. I also believe that you're one decision away from living your best life, so keep looking for that right move but remember it is a move for you.

"Don't wait for things to get better. Life will always be complicated. You need to learn to be happy now, and if you're anything like me, it's time to slow down to get there."

Slowly, in the last fifteen years, I have completely come to lose my identity and my purpose in life. I also bought into the glorification of busyness and "the hustle," all without knowing it. I bought into mommy wine culture, as well as the perfect families on social media. All these things added up in my mind and slowly caused me to make bad decisions, put the most important people in my life aside, put my values aside, and ultimately put my life in jeopardy. No matter what I did, it wasn't enough. Nothing made me happy. I had no emotions left because I was on repeat, trying to get to a place that never existed: perfection.

For so long I fit into everyone else's idea of who I should be, and I was so afraid of breaking that image, but it was making me miserable, slowly. I needed to break this learned behaviour and become the Marika who was around before she got lost in the hamster wheel of life these last few years. I needed that amazing girl back, so, in my fast-paced world of real estate, entrepreneurship, plus all the extra things added to my daily life, I made that one decision.

I remember lying in bed one morning earlier this spring and thinking about how much more energy, time, and money I was exerting on doing everything for everyone and "making things right" by fixing all the mistakes others made and fixing all the mistakes I had made. That energy could have been used for a greater purpose, maybe even to prevent the mistakes from happening in the first place.

The truth is, I was too busy doing all the things, and it was starting to take a toll on me. I would spend all day running around, maxing my mental capacity for dealing with people, and when the day was done, I needed to make myself feel better and that usually meant having a few glasses of wine to let the stress out. Everyone does it! If only I knew what it was doing to me. If only I took less on and had more balance. I can say "if only" as many times as you want me to, but it doesn't change anything.

That was the moment, in my bed that morning. Something clicked in my mind that day, and my purpose became greater. I knew I couldn't keep going that way. I wanted my emotions back, I wanted to feel healthy, and I wanted to go back to the girl I know I lost along the way.

That day, humility filled my soul. It was so powerful. For a perfectionist, humility is gold! Thank you, Universe! I felt so right in knowing what I had to do. This moment gave me the strength to stop working so hard at everything else and start working on taking care of myself. The decision was to figure out who I was, dissect this tricky situation I had created for myself, and figure out how the heck I was going to get out of it—a decision I should have made for my mental health a very long time ago but was scared to because I feared what people would think of me.

What happens when you are simply existing in life and not actually engaged or present? You become detached, your mentality burns out, and you don't pay attention to the details because there's just too much going on in your head. You don't pay attention to people, and you develop bad habits. Cue lost opportunities, rocky relationships, and more "fixing" of bad situations, in my case.

Burnout comes from chronic stress that is not managed properly. Imagine how much stress a person has trying to please the entire world, doing everything herself, working a demanding career, still being besties with wine, dealing ongoingly with a separation, and "momming" two children as hard as she possibly can. All while trying to look good and still be active on social media pretending life is so fabulous. Well, it's nowhere near fabulous. When you're that exhausted, your body and mind start to change, and you truly just cannot feel anything positive about your life because you don't have time to think of enjoying it. Detached and disconnected.

Take a small step back and look at your life. Think about your day-to-day. Think about all the things you do, the responsibilities you have, the people you touch, the bad and good habits you have, the work you do, the things that make you happy, sad . . . everything. What conclusion do you come to about all of it? Why do you do it? Is it rewarding or do you feel drained, maybe on repeat? I bet from the outside looking in, life seems close to perfect and typical for you, but to you on the inside, there is nothing perfect about it. It's a downward spiral to a breakdown.

When I ask myself these questions, I think of all the pressures society has on women. I think of stereotypes, and I think of social media. We've all seen that mom with three kids who does it all. She's a master chef, her house is always clean, she goes to the gym regularly, she has a kickass job or blog or something, and she has "mommy wine" playdates with the kids, all in a day! How do they do it all and still look great? That is huge pressure, and I am first to say I fell for it all.

When I realized it and even had an inkling to change my life for the better, the plan kicked in, in my head. I was motivated and ready to go! Number one, I needed to remove as much stress out of my life as possible. Number two, the wine had to go!

Imagine this: You're on a remote island having to learn a whole new way of life. Everything you were doing to "keep up with the Joneses" just stopped, and it was just you. Would you feel comfortable being alone? Since your hobbies diminished and you had no job, what would you do with your days? Scary, hey? Scary for me, that's for sure, and that is where I was at. I needed to stop everything and learn to be me.

I Am My Own Superhero

"You are the hero of our own story. The privilege of a lifetime is being who you are."

–Joseph Campbell, A Joseph Campbell Companion: Reflections on the Art of Living

I slowed down. I slowed everything down. I got out of my own way, and it was not easy. From being the ultimate multitasker, at the top of my game, striving for perfection that was never going to come, I had to lose this fear of letting everyone down. I had to lose the pressure I had on me from all the external sources.

I was aiming for perfection, but we all know that it doesn't exist. Perfection is abstract, and I had failed before I even started so many years ago. I knew it was time to turn this mess around because I didn't want to waste any more time!

The year 2021 was hard for me on many levels, but I do believe that our biggest failures teach us the most valuable lessons in life and letting things fall apart isn't the end of the world, it's a chance to rebuild it in a better way, and that's what mode I was in: the rebuild of my relationships, career, and MYSELF.

When you live quietly, and project humility, your mind is peaceful and nothing else matters.

Reflections

Before I could figure out what to do, I needed to figure out why I was this way. I truly called in the squad of help, and I will be the first one to tell you that asking for help for someone like me is very, very hard.

I learned that perfectionism is a form of addiction, and addiction is a symptom of leftover pain in our nervous system from experiences we've had that cause us to subconsciously escape our reality.

I wasn't only ever addicted to one thing. What I was addicted to was filling the void inside of me with things other than love, including (but not limited to) social media, alcohol, the hustle . . . anything to keep me from feeling alone.

Try watching a movie with me! My brain is never present because she's always thinking about the next best thing. I grab my phone, I stand up, I wander around the house, and I look for things to do when there is nothing else to do. It's a false reality I create to fill that void, and frankly, I have these irrational thoughts that I am not being productive if I am just sitting. I need to be doing something active to be productive. Well, that's all wrong! What happened to active rest days?

But there was more to this way of life I had created. First, there was the pressure growing up in a European household. Get good grades, go to university, get a degree, get a good job, do it this way, do it that way. Well, I did all that, but the truth is, no matter what I did, it was never good enough.

Is that why I strive for perfection in everything I do?

My life as a child was pretty self-sufficient, and I did a lot for myself, by myself, and maybe that is why I nurture my kids perhaps to a fault. I want my kids to be happy, and I don't want them to think they are not good enough, so with that, I have created what I never had. Sit-down meals together, a loving family dynamic with people who say I love you and mean it, more quality time together, and no pressure about what you're going to be in life.

Long story short, there's a mix of generational and cultural family dynamics growing up that led me here. Pressure from my parents and society's pressure on women was the misery of my downfalls but also a blessing in disguise because once I realized how delusional it all was, I was able to come up with a plan to change it all.

The Operation

What is more important for this chapter's sake is what I did to curb this craziness I have been living. Changing long-lived learned habits and the way of life that had me running around like an Energizer Bunny every day to a slowed-down state really deserves a huge prize.

It was time to find myself again and sitting with myself, talking things through, calming my own anxiety, letting go, forgiving myself . . . it's a process. But I started. I started this undertaking and called it the "stay the eff away from me" phase of my journey. I took a complete break from work, social media, and pretty much the entire world and everyone in it. I made a plan to keep a good routine, not drink any alcohol, live healthfully, walk every day, and read a lot.

After a few days of getting to know myself again, I created the "bring me back to life" phase where I replaced all the external factors like the news, social media, and people with things that grounded me—things I used to like to do before this identity crisis hit me: hiking, running, walking, spending quality time with my kids without interruptions, cooking, yoga, reading. I'd even watch movies with no distraction.

The first few weeks were awesome. I felt great about my decisions. Social media wasn't bothering me. I was doing healthy stress-coping things like exercising and reading a ton of personal development books. This gave me more time to actually think, and I realized that my mistakes were a cry. I was crying out for help, silently wanting someone to expose my mentally burnt-out nervous system, but that wasn't the answer. The answer was within me the entire time.

It took so much inner work to get here and to be at peace with a slower-paced life. Intentionally, on a daily basis, I focus on myself. That is something very new to me, but gosh, has it ever done wonders for my life. I love my daily routine and stick to it because I know what happens if I don't.

Learning that I am, in fact, an introvert was a huge feat. I now know that I need to recharge my batteries before I take on the world. I wake up very early so I can spend a good three to four hours by myself in the morning, working on myself and on what I want to work on.

I practice mindfulness with every little thing I'm doing. From the bites of food I take to the thoughts I have, I treat every single moment of my day as a mindful exercise. Thinking about every little thing you are doing will slow you down immensely, and you'll get to know yourself better during the process.

I love to cook, and I spend a lot of time in the kitchen. You don't know how often I used to add a little bit more of this, or a little bit more of that, just to try and make the food perfect when it was completely unnecessary. Sometimes I would even ruin my hours of work by adding "more."

Cooking helped me realize that this perfectionism is entwined in all aspects of my life. Now I notice it everywhere, and I am able to stop myself, and that's the key: notice and release.

I had to learn what my body needed and how I could lose the anxiety with my mind. I had to learn that being busy was not a badge. I also had to make myself rest. I wasn't distracted anymore, so it was much easier.

I actually had to re-find my hobbies again and figure out what my values were. All of it had been lost. I have continued to do the things that calm me and make me feel good. I guess nowadays we call that self-care, which is so weird to think about because since when did we stop caring about ourselves?

And there it was. Humility hit me so hard, and it's the best. I describe it as genuine contentment. My favourite feeling. All these things made me feel present, not busy anymore.

I was present, not perfect, and totally okay with it.

Living My Best Days

The universe has a funny way of pushing us to a greater being. For me, this comes in signs, and this year has been full of them. From being in the worst position in life, of my life, I have come out to the best position. Reborn! Like a new baby learning the ropes of life all over again. That's me!

I look back at all the things in my past and I am so grateful for all the mistakes I made, the failures I created, all the days and nights I put everyone else before ME. I am grateful that I ran myself to the ground every day in trying to be a super agent, super mom, and super woman, all at the same time! All of that has brought me here today, being able to tell my story and maybe affect just one person in a positive way.

Today, the word "more" is not in my vocabulary so much. I don't care what people think of me or my actions anymore. I don't care about what's going on, on Facebook or Instagram. I don't care if I don't get something done quickly, and I know that everyone else's life is not my business.

My fire is my resilience. My fire is my power, and once I forgave myself for my past, the true me came about.

This whole period of self-discovery could not have happened without letting everything stressing me out go away. I highly recommend it.

I have felt so much relief, so much humility, and so much clarity in the last few months. The only person I ever have to blame is myself. Yes, I am proud of myself, and yes, I feel great now, but life was not always full of daisies. Frankly, it still isn't, but what has changed is me, the way I look at things, and the way I take on the world.

"Not all storms come to disrupt your life. Some come to clear your path."

–Paulo Coelho

When I was approached about this book, I was secretly jumping for joy! My younger self always dreamed of being a writer, and wow, this was my first chance! I read the description, and I knew it was exactly what I needed, when I needed it. Not only was this a sign I accepted, but it was a perfect time to unload ALL that has been ailing me this past year. A cleanse.

So, I started to think about it. I am full of fire. My fire is my resilience. My fire is my power, and once I forgave myself for my past, the true me came about. Confident, happy, and respectful of myself and my body. Clear.

My fire is not complying with societal norms by creating this perfect housewife or perfect mom who does everything for everyone while working a full-time job with a huge smile on her face and looking like she is going to a dinner party every single minute of the day—full makeup, high heels, and all!

My fire is putting myself first. My fire is making the decision to change my life and not giving a fuck about what others think. That's my fire, and I am full of it!

You cannot put a bandage on your life and hope it gets better or that your feelings will go away. You need to deal with it head-on and make the necessary changes. I stopped my chronic overdoing. I stopped pleasing people because I didn't have to anymore. I WAS ENOUGH! I took ownership of my mistakes and made things right within myself.

The yearn for making more and more money is gone. That addictive personality of mine has learned minimalism, balance, moderation, calmness, sensibility, and self-respect. I am more real than I have ever felt, but it took major work—lots and lots of work.

This operation of mine has been one of my biggest accomplishments, and I am proud that I have made even more decisions to slow down my life and shift my business in a way that I can do more of me. That's what led me to this role of health, wealth, and happiness, and without this shift, I would not be here. Literally.

It's not about anyone else and what they think, it's about what makes sense to you. You do you.

I wrote this chapter to express how important it has been in my life to slow down and start living a more joyous, fulfilled life. I would like to wish that same contentment upon anyone who reads it and can resonate with what I was going through.

I have come a long way to become the woman I am today, and none of it would be possible without the love of my children, Nikolas and Kennedy, and the support of my partner and closest friends. I am deeply grateful for you all. I would also like to thank the other authors in our book for sharing their stories to inspire me and other women. Sky, you have been a great supporter throughout this process. Thank you all!

Marika Soleil is a woman on a mission! She took all the right steps to slow down the "busyness" in her life so that she could find her true self, and you can tell. With that, her goal is to encourage other women to do the same. Do the self-care, take a break, and stop putting yourself in a cookie-cutter picture of society's image of the perfect woman, because striving for perfection will never get you there. Perfection is abstract. Find your true self and love her dearly.

Marika is a veteran realtor living in beautiful Kelowna, British Columbia. She is a loving partner, mother, and an avid supporter of many social issues including mental health, addictions, child and youth wellness, and homelessness. Marika loves to give back to her local community.

Marika's passions lie in helping others, spending lots of quality time with her two children, running, yoga, travel, and cooking! You'll find her doing all the things that ground her. One of them is acting as the lead coordinator for The Kelowna Shoebox Project, a social initiative that helps women experiencing homelessness by providing gift-filled shoeboxes.

Chapter Five

My Blind Spot: Why Love Isn't Enough

Keli Carpenter

I chuckled as I sat across Marissa, listening to her account of what is necessary for me in a relationship according to the eighth house in my Evolutionary Astrology Chart.

We were only three minutes into my reading when she explained that my Sun Sign, Venus and Mercury, were all in the eighth house, which rules birth, death, sex, transformation, mysteries, and truth at the deepest of levels.

Her first question to me, almost as if she knew the answer already, was, "Do you help people transform or make changes in their life?"

"Yes."

She continued. "With Venus being conjunct your Sun in that house, it suggests that you value partnership with someone who can transform as well. You need to be in partnership with someone open to self-development and spiritual growth. It is almost a turn-on or a deal-breaker on the flip side. Mercury is in there too, which tells me you also want to talk about it. You want to do the work and have a dialogue about it with your partner. You can't be with someone who is just passing through, content with the surface/ordinary aspects of life—you need to be with someone who is consciously doing this deep inner work with you."

My daughter and I were laughing at this point. I declared in total agreement, "Yes, it is essential—it is a deal-breaker—hence why I'm not married anymore."

We all laughed at this revelation of truth.

She affirmed, "Perfect. Okay, since we are here, let's back up a house (the seventh house is marriage). Apparently, you have Sagittarius in your seventh house, so your partner also needs to be free-spirited, passionate, and fun-loving. You need someone who goes with the flow, not someone who is overly structured or who will constrict you or put you in a box."

She continued. "This is something to be aware of when you're attracting a partner because sometimes we think, *well, maybe it can work*, and we invest in areas we shouldn't, but I'm sure you already know that."

I smile and nod in agreement.

Marissa went on to speak about my blind spot (the twelfth house—the house of shadow, of enemy, of self-undoing). She asked me about my childhood and whether I felt the need to control things or was controlled and whether I felt that way in my marriage as well, repeating those same patterns from childhood.

As I listened to her words, I felt the impact of that validation.

My mom was a spiritual seeker and a beautiful soul. She was open and had a big heart, but she also had a very challenging side. She was equally controlling, manipulative, and abusive while I was growing up. While back then it was called dysfunctional, I now see that she suffered from mental health issues and was unable to process her past traumas. She was hurting and hurt people, hurt people.

As a child, on the one hand, I truly felt loved by my mom, but at the same time, her dark side was equally damaging and confusing. It was like walking on a tightrope between two worlds.

So yes, I agreed with Marissa 1,000 percent: not only was my mom very controlling, but I also had to control myself, working hard to keep the peace. So, I became the "good girl." I learned to do what I was told, even though it left me living someone else's idea of who I should be.

Later in life, after attending many intensive personal development programs, together and separately, she would speak about her patterns of behaviour as a parent as her "*Dr. Jekyll and Mr. Hyde.*"

This reading's wisdom not only described my childhood experience but, more than anything, it illuminated what I already knew to be true about my eighteen-year marriage and the reason for its demise.

When I first met my husband, I had already spent years in immersive and exposing personal and spiritual work, exploring the depths of my own healing and consciousness as well as learning from my previous experiences and relationships. I was at a point in my life when I felt good with myself and knew what I wanted: it wasn't what I might call a regular relationship—been there, done that.

I was looking for a soul-to-soul partnership to explore the mysteries of life in a playful and deeply intimate way—the kind of intimate partnership that both excites me and scares me at the same time.

And I wasn't afraid to communicate this or do the work to achieve conscious partnership.

I was clear that all relationships require work and there are no fairy tales. I was willing to visit the depths of the shadows because I know it leads to awakening. My who-was-to-be husband and I communicated and explored this idea of conscious partnership on all levels. The kind where both partners are willing to do the healing work and choose truth over our conditioned, limited, wounded, egoic parts of self that inevitably get triggered when entering relationships, growing families, and simply living life.

Even though we met in a personal retreat workshop and he had a mentor (the one leading the workshop), I wasn't blind to the childhood traumas that revealed themselves. As I paid attention in the days that followed, I found myself observing his "*I'm not good enough*" belief, both through his word choices and his behaviours. His childhood pain and shame lived deep within his outer container of confidence in his passions, his personal development path, and his understanding of spiritual truths.

Over the coming weeks as we continued to converse about the energy between us and my desire to sit exposed, vulnerable, and liberated in relationship, I was witness to more of the parts of him that didn't fully love himself. I knew it meant he couldn't fully love me or show up in a relationship the way we had intentionally explored. I also felt the deeper, truer love that was also present—the kind every woman craves to feel. I felt this pure potential viscerally in my body; I was able to experience the depth of pure, embodied love that leaves you feeling vulnerable and naked, yet empowered and alive.

Since the world is filled with people who don't truly love themselves and the fact that fewer still confess a desire to co-create a conscious partnership, we entered into a relationship. In the beginning, I was capable of holding space for healing and joining as well as for his emotional and behavioural patterns because they weren't about me—I saw him, I saw me, and I knew what was possible when you choose to do your conscious healing work. Since we had already spoken in-depth about our intentions prior to making any commitment to each other on any level, I felt we were both on the same page about what we wanted within a lifelong, soul-filled relationship. That wasn't a question, nor is it a question today—we wanted the same thing—that is for certain.

Where I later found my "blind spot" was in my disconnect between what it means to want something versus choose something, as well as the impact unintegrated shame has on everyone. Up until this point, I had worked hard to achieve certain accomplishments in life, so I knew what it meant to want something, choose it, then follow through with that choice.

Just because possibility and potential exist in any given relationship doesn't mean both people don't have to choose it. And not a casual choosing—a choosing as if your life depends on it. This choice has to be made not only with every fibre of your being, but it must be accompanied by an insatiable desire to meet your darkness and vulnerability—I mean why else are we here if not to experience the depths of unconditional love, playful, soul-expanding intimacy and what it means to be in purpose-filled, compassionate service to humanity as a whole? I felt clear in my desire, willingness, and committed choice. But I was blind to the idea that just because someone declares their love and desire doesn't mean they are also capable of choosing it.

The first three years were very challenging. Within our first year, I found myself pregnant. Welcoming our first son was actually an incredible experience where I truly felt supported by my husband, my personal practices, my awareness and choices.

However, just prior to that and what came after was honestly rather difficult. His dark dives into depression, anxiety, and anger were heavy and started to take a toll on me, especially as a new mom. He became overly controlling, manipulative, and always apologetic afterward. He openly expressed his shortcomings, shame, and desire to co-create what we both wanted. We would have truly open, clear, honest, conscious communication when he wasn't in those dark moments, but when he was in them, it was as if he were a different person who couldn't see the world the same way.

Without fully realizing it, I started to shut down from fear of these dark places: the emotional instability and failure to create a solid foundation for our growing family. I went into the same managing mode that I had as a child. I found myself walking on eggshells and trying to maintain the safe bubble to keep the peace. It might not have looked like I was struggling on the outside, as I still felt clear about where we were going and kept up a certain veneer. I was committed to working on the relationship and holding space for his healing, knowing that as he healed, he would then be all of who he was meant to be and therefore able to be there for me the way I needed and desired (and the way he wanted to be). In fact, I almost fooled myself because of how much I'm capable of holding. But I've learned that just because I can doesn't mean it is working or that I should.

Just before we found out we were expecting our second child, I was feeling the impact of the dysfunction, I was struggling, and I still believed in what was possible on the other side. He wasn't a bad person; he was hurting and yet another example of how hurt people, hurt people. As my trainer and mentor Gabor Maté says, "Anything that is 'wrong' with you began as a survival mechanism in childhood." My husband's childhood wounds and survival mechanisms that once kept him safe were now displaying as dysfunctional, toxic behaviour that I was experiencing.

Does that excuse the behaviour?

No.

But I was still in support mode, leaning into the possibility for healing and asking what he needed. What was he missing and how could I support him so that he could become all of who he was and therefore show up as the father, husband, and man both of us desired?

One of the things that kept me committed is that I had witnessed enough marriages end, with partners believing the grass is greener on the other side yet finding themselves repeating the same patterns. I made a commitment to my kids and myself to break the cycle, so I was there for the long haul.

When I was expecting our second child, I was asked to become a mentor in the personal development workshops my teacher and mentor ran. It was also the perfect opportunity for my husband's healing. I spoke to my husband, and he agreed to go through this ten-month program as a way for him to step closer into his truth so we could move into the fuller life we desired.

I remember at that time feeling desperate for support. What I was experiencing was bigger than my skill set and ability to hold anymore. I remember telling my mentor that I felt like an abused wife. Sure, I named it, but I was also still following a misguided belief (my blind spot) that if I could just heal more, things would change. Since I co-create my reality, what more could I look at and own?

Partway through the ten-month program, my husband quit. But by now I had a new baby, along with a toddler, and we were financially tender. I went into survival mode to protect my kids and everything that was good within our family. I saw my only option as working harder to help him help himself so I could find freedom from "him."

So, again I invested in helping him embark on his life's passion. I remember repeating once again, "If he was only living his passions, he would feel fulfilled and find his sense of belonging and purpose, and then I'd be able to finally focus on me." There was so much good within him to be celebrated. When he was stuck in his inner cave of shame and unworthiness, it tore us apart and left me feeling on my own.

I wanted it for him, for me, and for our (now) three kids. My biggest dharma in this world (outside being the change I want to see) is conscious parenting. I did years of deep work before having kids because of my experience in childhood—I saw the good and beautiful as well as the dysfunctional, hurtful parts, and I wasn't willing to pass on the same damaging patterns—I chose to break the cycle of trauma.

Knowing my husband's pain and suffering, I was aware that if I left, he would go into a downward spiral. I'd been through messy, manipulative divorces as a child, and I was not willing to put my kids through that, no matter how much I needed to sacrifice. Kids cope until they can't.

They didn't choose this; kids are the innocent ones in these dynamics. Even though I was feeling depleted, I was also strong (and I still held seeds of hope for change).

As the time went on, I became aware of my growing anger and resentment toward him for not showing up and choosing truth over self-loathing despite his awareness and desire. I knew my anger and resentment were not going to support what I truly wanted, so once again, I dove into my own healing and took responsibility for my part of this dynamic. I took some marriage courses. I learned how to forgive and feel the depths of my pain and grief around the slow crumbling of our marriage.

In this process of healing, it once again highlighted the fact that he wasn't choosing himself or the work; therefore, he wasn't choosing us (albeit not because he didn't want to). Shame is an insidious emotion left over from past trauma, leaving the person feeling they are flawed and unworthy of belonging. People can learn to love the darker parts and even fully heal them, but it has to be spoken about, not hidden. These dark emotions must be met, held, and unravelled, and no one can do it for you. I needed to let go, give back his 100-percent responsibility for himself and only focus on my 100-percent instead of trying so hard to work on our 200-percent of the partnership.

For the next couple of years, I returned to working with my same mentor and set a hard line about what was his to work on and what was mine. I made a powerful inner declaration to him: *I will not do the work for you. I will no longer want this more than you.* My husband had skills, knowledge, and awareness—he had the ability to choose—and all true partnerships demand it. I stopped dragging him along in hopes he would step into the vision that was really mine all along. I saw him for where he was instead of where I wished he could be or what I wanted (and was still hanging on to).

People can learn to love the darker parts and even fully heal them, but it has to be spoken about, not hidden.

During a similar awakening experience I had had prior to my marriage, I saw how clearly I had betrayed myself. In this opening, we actually both experienced a massive shift and felt we had been given a glimpse of what was truly possible—and maybe we had. But in the end, it was rather surreal witnessing him slide back into the darkness, dysfunction, and unconsciousness as I stood in awareness and in awe of how he could see what he saw. It was at that moment I knew

• • •

After eighteen years of missing my "blind spot" (my misdirected quest for conscious relationship) coupled with my lifelong understanding that what doesn't get healed repeats, I knew I had to lean into and unravel my own attachments if I was to fulfill this aching in my soul that had been unquenched as long as I could remember. I took the needed time to turn inward, let go, and listen until I was able to come to the place where I knew, like I knew, separation was the most loving, kind thing I could do for myself and my husband. I was setting us both free even though he couldn't see it yet.

At the end of my reading, Marissa asked me to pick a date in the future or past that I'd like insights about what was happening at that time. I thought for a moment—there weren't any dates I was overly curious about. Maybe my mom's death? Perhaps one of my children's births, but I have three, so which one would I pick?

I must interject here—at age six I was taught to practice Transcendental Meditation® and as I previously mentioned, I later attended (and then led) many in-depth, immersive personal development courses—essentially, I have spent a lifetime learning to listen to and for that quiet, intuitive voice of wisdom.

So as Marissa asked me this question, I heard that quiet yet knowing voice say, "The day you got married." I heard it and dismissed it, continuing to sift through dates in my mind.

She posed the query once again, and I heard that same voice of counsel say, "The day you got married." Having developed a deep relationship with this voice, I thought, "Okay, there must be a reason for it."

So, I said, "The day I got married: June 26, 1999."

As she typed, I almost felt as though I wasted one wish of three that the genie gave me. What would I need to know about that long past day?

Not a moment later, she started to chuckle. "Oh boy, are you ready? You're going to laugh. It was literally at that time that you were entering your blind spot; your twelfth house (the shadow and self-undoing). Saturn is already there (that's your restriction, shadow, and limitation), but Jupiter was just moving into that house as well. So, there was something beautiful about it too."

There was so much that came flooding in at that moment. It was as if my whole marriage made sense in a way that it hadn't before. This recognition was meaningful, as I have questioned at times how I stayed so long even though I was clear the whole time.

I jumped in with an unequivocal "yes." There was a lot of good, and the possibility for a conscious, loving partnership was pure. The light and the dark existed together.

This kind of present, aware uncoupling took a lot of dedication, commitment, and skill. But I wanted us both to celebrate what we shared instead of using it as fuel to stoke our pain and wounded narrative.

We lived in the same house separated and consciously healing for two years. As the world transitioned from 2019 into a brand-new year, my mom passed, my husband moved out, and I turned fifty all within a month of each other. There was pain, for sure, but I was also able to take a deep exhale in a way I hadn't done in a very long time.

It's taken my husband a bit more time to find a new level of closeness, as he still has attachments, but he is consciously working with his shame and now thanks me for making one of the hardest decisions I had to make for our family.

"Thank you for all the years you stood by me and gave to me and our family. And thank you for doing perhaps one of the hardest things in drawing the line and telling me to leave. It really was my wake-up call, and I understand that now. Ultimately, I wouldn't be who I am without you (along with the inevitability of it). You are the most amazing woman and part of my life. It truly breaks my heart to think of all the pain I caused the woman I love. All the hurt. All the times I let you down. All the times I didn't live up to my word."

Unentangling our relationship consciously has given us the privilege of maintaining our friendship. It has given our kids an example of conscious relationships and the power and safety that comes with true emotional healing. How many kids come from broken homes that are left managing their parents' volatile relationship for years to come? Together, we can now lean into this lifelong co-parenting relationship in amazing new ways—I was even able to stay at my was-band's house recently when I was in between moves, and it wasn't weird, awkward, or hard. I can appreciate our relationship instead of needing anything from it.

I may have been fully aware of my truth and what I wanted while willing to do my part. At the same time, I was conscious that I was trapped in this repeating story and trying everything I could to create transformation, but I still had a blind spot.

In the end, I had to choose me; this meant choosing truth over all else, even if that meant splitting up my family and hurting someone I loved. I had to risk all of who I am to become all of who I was meant to be. That is when I got to see the beauty in it all—when I got to realize a conscious relationship in spite of our separation.

No matter who you are, or what your story is, we all want to love and be loved without apology. I wanted to love, but I learned it's virtually impossible to love someone who can't allow love in. I wanted to be loved but know if someone doesn't love themselves, they can't really love you.

In the end, I needed to take off my blinders and love myself and my family enough to let go.

What I have learned through my conscious love journey is:

You are each 100 percent responsible for your 50 percent. Karmic contracts are between two people, and you can't take on more than what is yours. My commitment to make it work blinded me to my knowingness that it takes two to choose conscious partnership. You can't do the work for the other person, no matter how much you try.

Love is not enough. Love only matters when backed by committed, loving action. Wanting it isn't enough—the proof is in the pudding, not the promises and desires. You both have to choose to do the personal work if you want a conscious, loving partnership. Everyone is worthy of love, but our trustworthiness is based on our actions and is separate from our inner worthiness.

When someone shows you who they are, believe them. Mental health, personality disorders, or toxic behaviour are all a result of unintegrated trauma and require conscious, compassionate, skilled help; it's not your fault. Believe the love they have for you and believe them when they show you their limits to love. It is about their capacity to love, not how lovable you are. People can only love someone to the degree they can love themselves.

Be willing to risk everything for Truth. Speaking up and owning your truth is only as good as the boundaries that back it. Stay true to your voice. Choose you; choose truth always.

Support is essential. If we could have done it on our own, we would have already. Not all support is equal—there are therapists, friends, and family out there who are happy to support a wounded narrative, but true conscious support honours the pain without buying into the story that is keeping you stuck repeating the same patterns.

Kids are the innocent ones in relationships. Kids cope until they can't. As loving, mindful parents, it's our responsibility to heal so we can break the cycles of trauma and dysfunction. Helping our children experience inner fulfillment and confidence, to not be influenced by others, and to overcome life's inescapable obstacles only comes down to one skill set—the ability to listen to and trust our inner voice.

Shame and trauma are painful for everyone. Deep levels of shame bring feelings of being fundamentally flawed, mistrust, powerlessness, and worthlessness. As with all emotions, they are there for a reason. The shame isn't the gift, but there is always a gift in the centre when we have the right tools and support. If you struggle with shame, I invite you to find safe support and say, "Let's go there. Let's explore shame. Let's feel shame. Let's see what this shame is about."

My heartfelt thanks goes out to my (ex) husband for not only journeying through this story with me over the years but also for being there to support me through this writing process, even editing some of my grammar throughout my chapter. The sharing of my story in this format, I believe, has been another part of our healing (love) story.

I can't go without acknowledging my courageous seventeen-year-old daughter for sharing her story in this book as well. I'm not only bursting with pride, but this is something that will influence our mother-daughter connection forever.

Thank you, Mom, for being my teacher in more ways than you can imagine. I know your soul is at peace now, and I feel you with me always.

To my three kids (my greatest accomplishments), you are the very reason (the glue) that has kept me committed to serving Truth, day in and day out, so that I could support you to live your best lives.

Keli Carpenter is no stranger to mind, body, spirit awareness; her spiritual journey began at the age of six when her mother took her to learn Transcendental Meditation® (TM®).

Keli is the founder of *The Other Side of Average—Therapy for the Soul*. She is a Chopra Center Certified Transcendent Meditation Instructor as well as a Conscious Healing, Relationship, and Uncoupling Coach. Additionally, Keli is a Breathwork Facilitator and Mentor. Currently, she's attending Gabor Maté's Professional Compassionate Inquiry Training.

She helps conscious women learn the three most essential tools that align you with your soul's purpose—your essential nature and the truest expression of yourself while healing and transcending past resentments and stories that have kept you stuck and in pain. It's then that you experience the miracles and fulfillment of life in every moment.

This mom of three embodies all that she teaches; she doesn't just talk it, she *walks* it. Her chapter in this book is evidence of that (she has faced and overcome her doubts and fears about her writing alongside her healing journey).

Keli isn't here to be your guru but rather to inspire change and hold the space for you to bring light to your darkness, so you can reclaim the power you already have. It is about waking up to your true nature and realizing who you thought you were really wasn't the truth. It's all there within you; you are enough.

Chapter Six

Sex, Shame, and Obligation: What It Took to Become Unapologetically Me

Gaia Carpenter

What does it mean to become unapologetically you?

I think that's something we are all after. I think it's something we all long for; I certainly did. But most of us struggle with it for a variety of reasons. We're desperately worried about what other people think of us. We're even more worried about what they might think if they could see the real us. But . . . often we don't know how to be the real us. We don't really know what it means to be unapologetically ourselves.

Let's see if we can find out, shall we?

In this chapter, I will be sharing with you how I became unapologetically me. And . . . if I'm being honest, I'm still learning. But perhaps some of you will relate to me and what I've experienced in my own journey, and hopefully, I can help you own some of your own power through my story. Ultimately, however, that is a choice you have to be willing to make for yourself. So, let's start by finding out what it means to become unapologetically you. Ready?

For me, being unapologetically you is owning your power and stepping into who you are fully, even if other people disapprove. In fact, I'd say it's being who you truly are *especially* when they disapprove. For most of us, that can be exceedingly difficult. I was very worried about what others thought of me until I learned how to stand more in my power. I think most of us are so worried about being good enough or being accepted, that we'll often disguise who we really are in an attempt to belong.

In my experience, being unapologetically you is most definitely not being sorry, nor apologizing for who you are, what you want to do, and who you want to be. That being said, it can be easy to confuse who we truly are with ideas we have about who we are.

This includes brave actions such as speaking one's mind, for instance. While that can *seem* empowering, often what we're thinking can be reactive and hurtful, as well as distant from the truth of who we are. Becoming unapologetically you is certainly not an excuse to be rude to people unless they are putting you down and you feel the need to tell them where their place is. If I expand on my experience of the difference between standing up for yourself and being rude, standing up for yourself doesn't mean being a tyrant or being aggressive or yelling at people. To me, standing up for yourself is simply having confidence in the authenticity of your feelings and valuing your own worth; it's about owning your feelings by taking full responsibility for them, giving them a voice, and honouring what you need.

I've discovered that in order to become unapologetically me, I've had to give myself permission to say what I truly want and need. It also means finding ways to meet those needs without relying on other people for them. Recently, I've discovered that this might mean even doing what is unpopular. As a seventeen-year-old girl, in a society where not having sex at a certain age is weird and shamed, I have had my fair share of being shamed and have received numerous comments about not having had sex yet. But . . . what is the big rush?

Throughout this story, I will be talking about some memorable moments—both empowering and disempowering—that I've gone through and the feelings I experienced around these moments. And I'm fairly sure many of you have felt similar emotions and maybe even have had similar experiences. And well, occasionally, I still feel these emotions from time to time, as I'm sure you do also. But the critical thing I try to remember is to not get stuck in the story about why I'm feeling the way I am. Whatever that story may be and however justified it may seem, I've come to realize that the story needs to be relooked at for any false beliefs or perceptions and that my feelings are there to be honoured and felt fully.

I have gone through some very pivotal moments in my life so far, and I know I will go through many more. But, over time, I have learned how to say *fuck it* without actually saying the words (unless, of course, they were pertinent to the situation). But these moments were good learning experiences for me, even if I felt like shit after some of them. Even if I didn't see or understand the lesson right away.

For instance, I always knew I didn't have to finish school; I always had a choice. My family was okay with whatever decision I made, as long as I had a plan if I did decide to do life my way. Even though my mental health was at its lowest when I was in school, by hiding it from everyone, and always putting up a front, I ended up being genuinely good at pretending. Even though I was suffering internally, I stayed in school longer than what was ultimately right for me, because I had this romanticized fantasy about what it meant to be in high school. Eventually, I just ended up not being able to keep up the facade, so I made a plan. I have always known what I wanted to do in life: be a professional artist. So, I talked to my parents, and we found an art course with three stages: it teaches you different techniques, how to find your own style, and how to sell and market your art. So, I made the decision to quit school; I dropped out. I started my art course and began writing a book, and my mental health improved drastically; I felt so much happier and so much safer, even though I knew I had lots to still learn about myself and hurdles to overcome.

Almost a year to the day after making that decision, my mom got a message about this book where empowered women could come together and write their stories. Where they could share what it means to them to feel truly empowered and their journey against the grain to realize it. Because I so resonated with what the book was about, she asked me if I wanted to join; I was thrilled to hear the news (imagine being published for the first time at seventeen!) and was very excited to share my own story.

If you're willing to become unapologetically you, you will find the people in your life that are willing to love you for who you are.

So, right now in life, I'm writing two books and learning how to pursue my art career. I dropped out of school, I learned how to love myself and be who I am, and I'm just trying to live my life the way I truly want to, not how others want me to. It took me a few years to be where I am now, and quite frankly, I still have a long way to go; some days are better than others, but I am willing to learn and make mistakes along the way to becoming *unapologetically me.*

I find that if you're willing to become unapologetically you, you will find the people in your life that are willing to love you for who you are. I have friends and family who don't necessarily understand some of my choices, such as dropping out of school, because they believe that we need a high school diploma to be successful in life. And I bet some of you reading this now agree with that as well. And well, that is totally okay. After all, I'm not saying everyonc should drop out of school—if staying in school is what you want, stay. You do you and I'll do me. I'm just saying it doesn't dictate who you are. Nor am I saying drop out and be a couch potato. I'm saying do what you want to do in life and pursue it wholeheartedly. I'm saying don't tell me I will be unsuccessful in life because I didn't finish school. I'm saying many people are stuck in a job they hate and a life they don't want to live, and that's because we have been taught that you have to have a high school diploma and higher education to be successful in life (and to get a job). So, let me ask all the people that have a high school diploma, do you ever look at it? Do you find that it has helped you to live the life of your dreams and feel truly empowered? Has it helped you to be *unapologetically you*? If it has, that is truly wonderful. But if you don't feel like you are being unapologetically you—the empowered you—what would it actually take for you to be *that*? Many very successful/famous people dropped out and/or never even went to school. And yes, many people aren't successful, but that is because they either gave up when it was hard, or they never even tried to begin with. So, what I'm saying is, let's agree to disagree. Let's let each other be who we truly want to be.

Even if my friends disagree with that choice (to drop out of school), they still love me, and I still love them. They are still here for me, and

I will always be there for them. And to be honest, no one will stop me from being who I am anyway. I will not be shoved into a box!

I've had so many pivotal moments that have helped me learn what it means to become unapologetically me.

There have been countless times I have been shamed for not having had sex yet, but this one incident continued to play in my head for some time. I was hanging out with a few of my friends and some of our mutual friends. We were at a mutual friend's house; this mutual friend regularly shames me about something when we all hang out. It's usually about sex. This one particular time, it was a little overboard. Three of us were in her living room: me, her, and a guy. The two of them ended up talking about sex as they often do; no problem with that. Then, out of nowhere, she turned to me and asked me a question about sex in front of this guy (knowing I have never had sex). Right after asking the question, she goes on to say, "Oh, wait!" Laughter. "I don't even know why I'm asking you; you've never even had sex."

The condescending way she said it made it obvious that she was trying to shame me in front of that guy. To top it off, every time she shames me, it has been in front of a guy she either likes or she's liked in the past (maybe to make herself look cooler?). And I just sat there and took it. I didn't say anything; I didn't do anything. I sat there and felt like shit; I sat there thinking, "I'm so lame that I haven't had sex yet." I sat there and thought of how ashamed I felt. I sat there and thought about how weird I am. I sat there and felt offended. I sat there and felt put down. I sat there and felt humiliated. I sat there and I felt hurt. I sat there and felt angry. I just *sat* there. This wasn't the first time something like this had happened to me, but I was so shocked I didn't know what to say or do. I even gave off a chuckle. And I know, for sure, that many others have stories like this or worse. These experiences often leave us thinking bad things about ourselves, like "I'm not enough," etc. When you really stop to think about it, why should anyone feel bad for not having sex? Why is that shameful? Why is there a rush?

Well, even though I have had experiences like this and ended up feeling bad about not having sex, even though I didn't stand up for myself then and there, I refuse to let anyone push me into having sex before I am ready.

I may still have to learn how to stand up for myself better, but I won't give in.

I know way too many people that had sex before they were ready, feeling like they had to and feeling shame around it. Feeling *obligated* to. Feeling pressured to. Then there's even more guilt or shame because they didn't listen to themselves.

Isn't it interesting that you can feel shame whether you do or whether you don't?

If you feel shame about not honouring your body, it doesn't mean you can't find your strength and take back your power, no matter how old or how young you might be. Everyone has a choice: you can take back ownership of your body and who you are!

And just like sex and how you can get shamed for not having had it yet (which is mind-boggling to me), it can be the same with many other things, like not drinking or not smoking. And well, frankly, I don't do either one of those things. And not because I'm not allowed, just because I don't like the taste. Even though that's considered weird and embarrassing for many people around my age, I've learned over the years to stand my ground and not give in—to remain steadfast to what feels right for me.

Even writing about all of this is another step into owning my power. Along the way of writing my story, I have thought a few times that I sound lame. But quite frankly, I'm not; I'm writing a *book*, for god's sake!

My brothers have thrown many parties that involved both drinking and smoking—like any other party. And yes, I go to these parties but don't do either one of these things. At first, I felt awkward and unwanted at these parties, but not by my family—they always made me feel welcome. I did still feel like a burden, however, especially to others. I felt shameful, I felt like a freak, I felt like a weirdo. I felt lame; I felt not "normal." What even is normal? I would hate it when people would find out I wasn't drinking or smoking; their reactions were unbearable; they would be in awe and just stare. Some of them would say things like, "OH, WOW, you don't drink?" or "That's weird," or when I haven't seen a person in a long time, and they say, "So you still don't drink? Hmm. What about smoke?"

Why do I need to do anything? Why is it weird if I don't do these things? Can't people have fun and hang out *without* drinking?

At first, I would pretend I was drunk; I got so good at it no one would realize that I wasn't. If someone found out I wasn't drinking, I would still feel embarrassed, so I wouldn't tell anyone and made it seem like I was drinking. Eventually, I moved more and more into my power and felt like it was okay not to drink. Now, I no longer pretend to be drunk, I just know how to have fun without alcohol. The responses of the people around me didn't change, but I did.

I don't care anymore if people know that I'm not drinking or smoking. I *own* it.

Many people do it because it's a social thing; it would be weird for them not to do it, even if they don't like it. I wonder how many people think the same way. I wonder, does anyone truthfully like drinking for the sake of drinking? Or do they do it because it's a social thing or because they feel pressure? Or because they want to escape something in their lives they don't want to face?

I felt like I would be a loner if I didn't do what everyone else was doing. That I needed to drink, smoke, and have sex in order to be liked by people. Or I felt peer pressured to do so, to impress the guy I liked. But, ultimately, liked by whom? People that won't accept all of who I am? So, I have to put on a fake facade? But that is just simply not true. People will show you who they are if you are willing to see them. And you will find the people who embrace you for who you are, even if they do things you don't. But the difference is they don't shame you for not doing those things, they just simply don't care. They like you for you.

There was another time I was caught in a social experiment and didn't know until after it happened.

One day, when I was still in school, I was walking to the bathroom, not necessarily because I needed to go, but because I needed a quick break. I was then stopped by a woman teacher. She asked me what I was doing and if I was willing to answer some questions. I was very hesitant because I was shy at the time, and I didn't have the inclination to do it. I wanted to say *no* but didn't want to be rude. But just because you say no to something, that doesn't mean you are being rude. It is harmless scenarios like these that help you practice how to say no. Even though this was a good learning experience for me and I don't regret doing it, there is something to be said for just saying no. Anyway, I ended up saying *maybe.* She asked again, saying *please.* I decided to say *yes*, thinking she'd send me back to my classroom to ask my teacher. Then instead of asking my teacher, I could just simply return to my class and avoid her. So, I said, "Yes, but I have to go tell my teacher."

She responded, "Don't worry, I'll tell her." (Plan foiled).

I ended up going into a room not knowing what I was about to do.

This room was tiny with one long table and about six guys, only guys, sitting at it; there was also a male teacher. To make matters worse, the female teacher left. I knew some of these boys; they were the kinda guys who were loud, annoying, and made rude jokes. I wasn't good friends with these boys, but they were all good friends with each other. So, I sat down, and the teacher presented a bunch of "which stick is longer" type questions for everyone; you know—the straightforward type of questions, but you think it's a trick question because it's so easy. He started handing them out one by one, and each of us, in turn, would answer out loud. They were certainly uncomplicated; one of us even asked, "Is this a trick question?" The teacher said *no* so we answered them; initially, we all gave the same answers. But after a while, the boys' answers changed. They began saying the smaller sticks were longer; I was getting a little confused. Some of them began to laugh, so I just thought they were joking around since I knew they do that a lot anyway. I kept confirming which one was the longest. The teacher, meanwhile, spoke to the boys, telling them to take this seriously (because they were laughing). I wasn't laughing; I didn't know why they were. But I started to question myself, thinking they were laughing *at* me because I had a different answer, and it was the wrong answer. For the most part, I kept my ground. Some questions were more complex than others, even though they weren't hard; in fact, there were two questions I answered wrong based on what the guys answered. I then thought to myself, *Why am I answering the same as what they are? They're just messing around.* So, I went back to answering which ones I knew were right, even though they were all saying something different. It went on for a while longer, then when we were finished, the teacher told me, "Thank you for taking this seriously." I replied, "You're welcome," then left the room. As I went out, I saw the other teacher standing outside; she came up to me and explained what the situation was about. She said, "This was actually a social experiment to see if you would be intimidated by all the boys and say the wrong answer because they were saying it, even though you knew the right answer." The boys were in on the experiment! I was the only one out of the loop. Even though I felt confused, for the most part I didn't say the wrong answer based on what the guys said. After realizing this, I felt happy and revived. I felt *strong*. In reflection, I really appreciated that I listened to myself.

Now, don't get me wrong. I still struggle with standing in my power; I am still discovering how to become unapologetically me. But I've learned not to allow others to put you in a box you can't really fit in. Or to even allow yourself to do so. Sometimes, I've found, our worst critic is *ourselves*.

I feel very lucky to have learned many useful tools in my life at such a young age. My mother introduced me to breathwork and meditation from the time I was very little, but I wasn't a huge fan of either of them until I became older. Those tools, along with being able to talk to and be vulnerable with her, helped me work through pain and supported me in developing a strong sense of self.

Even though I am still growing into who I am, these tools will ultimately help me be who I am in a world filled with people so disconnected from their true self. I am extremely grateful to have such courage and confidence in who I am at this age, while I'm still growing and learning.

So that is where I was: A teenager who felt sad, useless, unwanted, and sorry. A freak—put down, lame, and bleak. A weirdo.

This is where I am: I am doing things that make me feel happy. I am surrounding myself with people who accept me for who I am. I'm learning how to take ownership of who I am, and I'm learning how to stand up for myself. And, of course, I'm most definitely learning to pick my battles and tell people off when I really feel the need to do so!

This is where I'm going: I will learn to be unapologetically me utterly and completely. I will have some challenging moments, but I am willing to learn from them. I will do the things I love with the people I love who also love me. I will pick my battles when I really need to. I will feel no shame in who I am. I will give myself permission to speak up when I need to.

I will just say *fuck it and be me unapologetically.*

Who's going to join me?

I would like to acknowledge my father, Shawn, for the hours he put in to help me with editing and being supportive along the way. And to my mother, Keli, for coming along this writing journey, with whom I am very grateful to be writing my first book with. To my brothers, Dakota and Corbin, for supporting me and cheering me along when I didn't feel like writing. To all my friends: Anjelina, Estella, Carrera, Ellie, Rachel, Chelsea, Kaia, and Megan, for encouraging me and believing in me, even when I didn't, who are also excited to read the book. To every person in my life who has contributed to my learning experiences, even the people that I felt challenged by. To my editors for all the help along the way and for not giving up on me, even when I was a little late on doing the things I needed to do.

Gaia Carpenter is a bold, courageous young woman. This seventeen-year-old creative is an avid and aspiring wordsmith and artist. Having been enthralled with mazes, patterns, and sounds her entire life, Gaia's creative urges started even before she could put pen to paper.

When Gaia was young, she was always singing and drawing — she was constantly creating. In fact, she would often get her mom to scribe the songs she composed. This natural creative rhythm also came through in the poetry she would write; looking back throughout her childhood and teen years, there is no doubt she was born to be an artist!

An adventurous soul, Gaia is fulfilling a long-time dream of owning and renovating a mini school bus with her mom with the intention of using it to travel throughout Canada, attend festivals, and fulfill a piece of her bigger dream of travelling the world. Gaia is presently enrolled in a year-long professional art course and is authoring her first novel. After having been enrolled in a school for the arts and having been represented in a local art gallery on a few occasions, Gaia is both excited and honoured to be published alongside these empowered women, with her very own mom being one of them.

Chapter Seven

Running

Shelly Hope

This day is finally here, my stomach is flip-flopping and I want to jump up and down, but I'm being watched closely by the elderly man who decided to give me a chance. I'm not sure if I'm going to puke, scream, cry, or maybe a bit of everything, so I do nothing and instead put all my focus on breathing steadily. I reach for the keys from my new landlord's hand, scooping them up so quickly that I hardly touch his skin; it is as if the keys had been levitating. I shove them in my pocket, holding them tight, feeling the firm cold metal gouging into my palm, all the edges and curves being memorized by my fingertips. I slowly walk up the hallway to number four. The beige door has paint chips curling and peeling, revealing past colours of green and sky blue. Some of the wood is exposed; you can see where stickers had once been, their outlines still defined, yet it's the most beautiful door I have ever seen. I feel light with giddiness, leaning on the worn wood as I place my hand on the metal doorknob.

I remember the last time I decided to flee my family home. I had been running, and I looked down at my socks, soaked and covered in mud, my toes numb from the cold. The new rule was that no shoes were to be left at the front door because I kept leaving the house when the yelling started. We now had to take off our shoes and carry them down the stairs and place them onto the new shoe mat in the basement hall. This rule was told to us at supper one evening after I had left to avoid any outbursts. I remember I had been glared at, daring me to say a word in protest. I chose to say nothing, knowing that anything I'd say would be treated as an attack against the household rules.

The days I struggled at home exhausted me, and I would escape to the forest. I would wander back out of the comfort of the trees slowly, dragging my feet and feeling my shoulders tighten. I felt sad and defeated about having to go back. I realized that I had no choice; I needed to find a way to change my living situation, as I could no longer live in that environment. I needed to find a place where I could slowly peel back the layers of who I had become and had to be to survive. I needed to find a space where I could unbecome and learn to be me.

I slowly slip the key into the lock and turn. I take a deep breath. I don't want to rush this moment and yet it can't come quickly enough. I want to dance in the bathroom and sing in the kitchen, claiming every inch and every corner of it as mine, exploring and discovering the back of each drawer and cupboard and crack in the plaster. This is what I've been working toward for years, hoping and praying to whomever was listening—if anyone is listening—that one day this would happen. I stand there savouring the moment, equally wanting and not wanting to jump through the door from the stained hall carpet to the shiny hardwood in the apartment entrance, as well as partially wanting to skip through with uncontrollable tears of joy.

All the sacrifice, hard work, and perseverance has finally brought this moment to fruition. This is my new home. No roommates to clean up after, no loud kids running around, no family of strangers, no anyone, just me. I am responsible for everything that happens on the other side of this door. The bills, the cleaning, what kind of music I play, when and what I eat, even the colours I choose to paint the walls, if I even choose to paint them. I finally have a home all my own. I can smell the mustiness mixed with stale nicotine and boiled potatoes before I fully open the door. I'm thrilled to clean and unpack. Part of me wants to tell everyone that I did it, yet I still have to hook up a phone line.

I don't need a sixteenth birthday party next month. I have everything I've ever wanted right here at this moment. In order for this to happen, I had to believe in myself and stay true to my goals. I was told by almost everyone that I was too young to live on my own, that it was not possible at my age, that I was not responsible enough, and that it was going to be hard work. I kept responding that I could do it and that I was fully prepared to embrace all the challenges. I could move back home, but I knew it wasn't a healthy place for me. The dysfunction was not something I could survive any longer. I know all people have their issues to be aware of and work through, yet I could feel my heart slowly going cold and my thoughts becoming very dark and often scary. I felt like I was drowning, unable to get a hand on anything solid, slowly suffocating as time went on. The explosive behaviours of others were affecting my mental and physical health. I loved those in the home, yet I had to go. I felt obligated to be true to my intuition, true to my needs and to the voice within that whispered in the quiet, RUN!

When I was a little girl, I spent many hours and days alone. My parents lived in different towns, and I lived with my adopted dad during the school week while my sisters lived with my mom. My dad worked all day, so I had a key on a pink shoelace around my neck to unlock the door to our small two-bedroom house. It was my job to start supper and my homework before he arrived home. We would eat supper together and watch the news and then, in the evenings, my father would do paperwork and I would play in my room or outside in the lush forest behind our home. He never had to worry about me; the town's population was under 500 and everyone knew everyone. If my friends and I were causing trouble, then my dad would get a phone call from a neighbour. I just had to be home before the streetlights came on, and I usually was. This was how life was from grade one to grade six.

In grade seven, both households decided to live together, drastically shifting the family dynamic. All of a sudden, I was living with a large family that seemed more like strangers. The house was full of hormones, with teenagers and two stressed-out adults. I wasn't used to having to ask permission to do anything, as I had grown up with my father's trust to know what I was allowed to do. I wasn't accustomed to needing approval to do things or waiting to get approval. I had been taking care of myself with very little supervision, and I liked the freedom I had at my dad's house. I was accustomed to my independence, so I struggled with being controlled and explaining what I was up to. The household became more and more tense as we all tried to get to know one another. The arguing started to become a daily thing, and it wasn't long until the yelling became something more. By the end of grade seven I was hiding under large clothing the signs of what was going on in the home. I wouldn't change in the changeroom in front of others for gym class, and I was leaving lots of space around me so no one would see the bruises. I was ashamed and scared, and I started to pull away from the friends I had made when I first moved there.

I started to feel trapped and wasn't adapting well to this new situation, so I began taking solace in the forest around our new home, wandering at first for an hour or two and then more often and for longer periods of time. Spending my time in the woods at the end of our road was the one place I could go, and I knew no one would come looking for me. There were hundreds of acres of forest to explore with dozens of unmarked trails. I would walk for hours on end, just me and my dog, learning all the different hydro lines and trails, never running into another person. I would bring a backpack with snacks and water and dry socks and an extra sweater in hopes of maybe finding a spot where I could stay. I'd fantasize that I'd find a magical cave, hobbit house, or an abandoned hunter's cabin, but that never happened. Some days I would nap under the trees and wake up confused by the sensations of being wet and shivering from the cold. The smell of rain would envelop me, and I'd notice the wet seeping through my pants and the drops of rain landing on my head from the leaves and the rough bark against my back making my sweater stick to my skin. Other days, in the warmer seasons, I would pick berries and think about how people used to live off the land, and I'd start working on my edible plant identification skills. I loved listening to the birds fly low from one tree to another as they soliloquized. I would close my eyes, trying to hold that feeling for as long as I could. I felt welcome there; that was peace—the peace I craved and needed to survive. Sometimes my family wouldn't notice how long I was gone, and other times I was told to stop wandering in the forest due to the bears in our area and the real fear of me getting lost and them not knowing where to start looking. It confused all of them how I could amuse myself with so little for so long and not be fearful of the dark. In the forest I always felt so light. The birds were quiet except the few in the far-off distance, and the coyotes howled. There I was safe. There I could take deep breaths. There I was allowed to just be me.

My family reluctantly allowed me to move in with my grandparents in the city to get the math credit I needed to continue to stay in my grade after I had failed due to poor attendance. They also wanted to keep me away from the friends I had grown accustomed to hanging out with who were older and never went to classes. I had skipped grade four, so failing or being held back wasn't an option to them due to me allegedly having "so much potential." The word *potential* makes my skin crawl as though it's my life goal to become something for someone else, as though I'm not enough unless I impress the world and compete to be the best at whatever it is that people with so-called potential do.

It excited me to not only be in a new town, a small city even, but also to live with my grandparents who always respected me and never yelled or made me feel small. Their love was warm and I craved it, plus my grandma was an amazing cook and baker, so that was a bonus. I was excited to meet new kids, be somewhere different, and to get away from my depressing, tiny town full of alcoholism and poverty. It took half the summer to convince my family to continue to allow me to stay with my grandparents in the fall, promising to go to school and to get good grades, to be respectful and to never skip school. That gave me the freedom I needed to start fresh, to not feel disempowered and fearful with every breath, and to no longer live in the shadows.

I left my grandparents' house a few months later, however, because my family told me it was time for me to come back home. My grandparents said it was okay for me to stay and enjoyed having a kid in the house again, but my family said they missed me and that this situation wasn't necessary because they said that if I can thrive at my grandparents' home, I can thrive back in the family home. I didn't want to stay at my grandparents' house anymore in fear of causing a more negative family dynamic between the generations. I could see it in my grandma's eyes that it was breaking her heart, and I felt responsible for putting her in that situation. But I refused to go back like I had the other times, just to return, hoping something had changed. I began to seek new places to stay, knowing lots of kids from taking one semester of grade eleven in the community. I continued to visit my grandparents weekly to catch up, and they took me grocery shopping to make sure I had something to eat. They also knew that sometimes I slept outside if I couldn't find a place to crash. I felt closer to them and thought of them more as parents than grandparents at this time.

I guess it was starting to show by the middle of grade eleven that after being in survival mode for so long that I was no longer functioning as a healthy teenager. I was not thriving; I was only getting good grades again. I was having explosive moments in classrooms, and the anger was seething out of me at every moment. I was placed into a weekly anger management class at school for at-risk youth. At first, this group seemed like a joke, a round table of misfit girls, everyone hating each other and eyeing one another with suspicion, but we got out of classes, so we all attended religiously. And then slowly something happened. I started to trust and open up to my counsellors, sharing all the secrets I could no longer keep. They were the ones who told me after many months in group about a government program that helped youth just like me. The only issue was that I would have to get my parents to sign a paper stating that they would no longer financially support me because I was under sixteen, and that was the law in our area. I hadn't lived in their home full time for over two years, but they still had to sign the paperwork. I didn't think they ever would, but finally with my grandparents' influence, they caved in with the knowledge that this was my opportunity to find semi-permanent housing instead of choosing to be on the streets full time. Disapproval was expressed by those around me who didn't fully know what I was dealing with or why I was allowed to become responsible for myself. It was just a matter of months before I had been given money to get my own place, so I worked at exhausting all the couch-surfing options I could find until then. The school guidance counsellors also supported me in the choice to become a fully independent youth. They knew my behaviours were clearly not an act, as they could see the suffering I was going through due to trauma.

I moved a few times the first six months, trying out different living situations because the money I was given monthly was a very small amount. At first, I rented a place where you could rent a bedroom and share a bathroom and kitchen, then I rented a room from a friend's family, and then another. That was okay for a while, but it never really felt like a home when living with another family and hearing their arguments and struggles. It triggered me to self-harm. I would lock myself in my room for hours and hours, just trying to get some peace and quiet. Then I got a part-time job and it allowed me to look for my own place, to find a small spot just for me.

The apartment I chose was perfect. It was tiny and affordable, and it was close to downtown where I worked. The kitchen was the size of a small closet with a cute miniature oven/stove. I didn't care; it was all I needed. Most of my cooking was basic, and I didn't need a large kitchen. It had a little deck, a big bathtub, and hardwood floors, and I instantly loved it. In order to afford this space, I had to work every day after school for a couple of hours and full Saturdays. I didn't mind if it meant that I got the freedom of having my own place; I would do whatever it took to finally have a comfortable home. Evenings were long. I would make my supper after work and sit with my goldfish to eat. There was no one to talk to or to share my day with, but then I got used to it and enjoyed the most welcomed silence. I enjoyed my own company more and more. I used my extra money from my second job to decorate, I learned how to cook a little bit better, and I watched movies, read, and listened to music while passing the evenings away. I did struggle with friends at this time; they all lived with their parents and always had to ask permission to do everything. With no adults at my place to watch over us, some of my friends weren't allowed to come over, even though we weren't doing anything that other normal teens weren't doing. My friends would complain that their moms didn't do their laundry so their favourite jeans were dirty, or that their fathers wouldn't give them the car that weekend, or that an annoying little sister was using their makeup. I didn't have these issues, and I felt alienated quite often. I don't think they realized that in order to have this apartment, I had to do everything on my own at every second. If I was stuck on a math equation or had an argument with a friend, I had to try and come to a solution on my own. I had no sister to chat with, no dad to joke around with, no mom to show me how to fix my bad hair, and no dog to snuggle and run into the woods with. If I was sick, I had to make my own soup and drag my butt to the local drugstore for cold medicine. If a piece of my school uniform needed replacing, I had to budget tightly to still pay the hydro bill. Living without mistreatment was obviously worth it but learning to be a strong and healthy adult was harder than I thought. My friends romanticized having their own place and never saw how hard it was. I just kept putting one foot in front of the other and figured if I just finished high school and kept paying my bills, everything would

If we don't work at actively healing, then we pass on our trauma to those we interact with.

be great, all the hard times would be behind me, and there would be nothing but good in my future.

I read what to do to become a mentally and emotionally healthy person in books and magazines, and I did all those things religiously, yet the results were rather chaotic. I didn't have anyone with experience to talk to, and my anger management classes at high school had ended. I figured I had the tools to cope with life, yet the darkness was seeping in more and more. I started to skip meals, and I began cutting myself again like I had begun doing in junior high. I hadn't cut myself in almost over a year. I felt angry, ashamed, and sad because of my behaviour. I joined a gym and started to look for perfection in my body, consumed with size and numbers. I developed an unhealthy obsession with working out, no matter what level of exhaustion I was dealing with. I constantly kept thinking that health was a checklist and to stay the course.

I decided to speak to the counsellors at school and started to see someone again. This time it was one-on-one therapy to help me understand what I was going through and to process my trauma. I needed help again, not realizing that healing was a lifetime goal. Depression kept slowly creeping in. Then suddenly I felt huge waves of panic, and this feeling was happening almost daily. At first, I thought maybe I had a mental illness, knowing mental health issues are clearly in my bloodline. I went to my doctor who said that it was anxiety and it was common, that I had to learn to take deep breaths, and who gave me some tools on how to deal with it when it came. I often woke up sweating in the middle of the night, heart racing. I would reach to turn on the bedside lamp, then I'd calm myself down and go through my breathing exercises and try to get back to sleep. I started to meditate and make healthy meals, and I went to bed early so I could feel well the next day.

When I was a little kid, I always thought that adults were perfect—they knew all the answers, being wise with age, and I was excited to one day be an adult with this unlimited knowledge. Then, as I got older, I began noticing that this may not be the case. If we don't work at actively healing, then we pass on our trauma to those we interact with. Growing up, I had large parts of my life that were sad and depressing, and it was my job to work through these times to heal. I didn't cause the pain, but it was mine, and I could decide what I was going to do with it. I needed to be told that it's okay to make errors, that being a teenager can be difficult, that I was awkwardly awesome, and that I should keep being my weirdo self. Instead, I had to be the best at everything I participated in and get all straight As. I demanded perfection from myself, just as I had been taught. The pressure was too much, and I also didn't want any of it. I chose to try my best to let go of the pain from the experiences, as this wasn't my baggage to carry, and learning to release it was my task to becoming my own person.

That first day at the apartment door, with my name on the mailbox, was the start of something so huge that I didn't even know it at that moment. I am thankful for following through with the need to leave and find my own place in order to thrive and heal. All the struggles and challenges were worth it to learn what my strengths were and to grow as an independent young adult. Wishing and daydreaming weren't going to bring any change to my situation. I had to take action. I stayed at that cozy home for three and a half years, and I often yearned for that level of peace and privacy in my late teens and early twenties. I worked toward healing, but I would sometimes find myself choosing poor romantic partners and friends, eager for love and approval, no matter what the price. I still wasn't able to fully believe at the time that I deserved to be treated with respect and love. My struggles would show up repeatedly until I learned those lessons and they became a part of my core beliefs. I now know that we create our fate through our choices, and that this is my life to choose. My happiness and joy are up to me. No matter where I move, I always think back to that day I had the keys to that apartment in my hand, and I could finally stop running.

Shelly Hope likes to wear black hoodies and talk to the trees under the light of the moon. Dogs are her best friends and snow makes her giggle. She loves to travel with her life love, consume all the books possible, and teach yoga.

Chapter Eight

Lessons Learned

Shae Lemire-Cochrane

It won't matter how loud you love if the other person isn't listening. First lesson.

I fell in love. Hard and fast. Head over heels, didn't think about it at all, only felt that incredible chemistry, that zing, that intense like and dislike depending on the circumstances, and I thought, *how can I feel this strongly for someone and it not be love? This is greater than anything else I've experienced yet, isn't it?* There were signs, I saw them, but I just didn't register them because I also wasn't yet in tune with my emotional intelligence. Nor did I realize that there was one other major problem: our core values were not aligned.

Our relationship was a whirlwind romance. We met online, lived in different cities and drove back and forth, more and more recklessly in love until we moved in together. Looking back now, it seemed fast, but it was such blind chemistry, and we were in that same "looking for a mate" stage of life. I met his parents, and his mom and I zinged almost as much as my boyfriend and I did; we just "took" to each other immediately. She was a beautiful, kind-hearted woman, who saw the best side of everyone. She'd always tell me how special I was when she'd stop by and I'd be landscaping in the yard, cleaning the house, or making a nice meal for the end of the workday. She babysat our dogs when I worked, and I'd drop them off to her and pick them up every morning and evening, thankful for our relationship. My connection with her was as important to me as my connection to her son.

The honeymoon stage continued while being introduced to all his friends. Generous, flattering words poured all over me; they beamed happiness and approval at me. My heart was always racing when we were together, and I remember the excitement of feeling like I'd finally found my person. Another six or so months later, we were moving into our first house. It was in that house where I noticed red flags, but after communicating my needs, I would be left with just enough to hope and believe that reciprocation, ego sacrifice, and personal growth changes could and would be made sooner rather than later.

Just a few years down the road we were married, and after just barely four years together, we finally conceived a child. I say "finally" because during those four years, I had been told I had undiagnosable infertility, and we had basically given up on the idea of children. I know now that it was stress over the already troubled relationship. But back then, I was mostly just too scared to ask for feedback or help about it, thinking it was the normal "ups and downs" in a relationship. I reached out within the family unit a few times but was basically told that "this is the way it is," and I guess I just took their word for it. As it would eventually happen, I was actually at an ultrasound to see why I wasn't getting pregnant when I found out that, just by a few weeks, I already was. My pregnancy was complicated from the beginning to the end, ravaging my body, but it gave us our beautiful child.

More chances to open up to my self-awareness popped up here and there when our child was just an infant. My father-in-law was dying from cancer and told me the relationship wouldn't last because I was not someone who could be controlled. He had said this same thing once before when his son and I were dating, and it didn't register because I wasn't yet able to process the cycle I had jumped into. At the time, I didn't have the strength to look into the heart of what he was talking about. I told myself he was a dying elderly man, and my relationship would outlast him and his words. However, he was a perpetrator in the unhealthy cycle I had fallen into, and he fully recognized that, I now know.

Then the undermining started, but it was irregular because of our lifestyle and therefore not obvious to me at first. Originally, when we met and talked about children and family, it was a simple conversation; I would be home raising a child while his superior wages provided for the family. It was the example set in our childhoods, my point of reference being somewhat similar. My father worked while my mother stayed home with my brother and me until I was eight, but then my childhood became quite traumatic, as my mother had to leave my father after years of abuse. I only knew that if I were having a child, I wanted to make sure that the little one would be raised at home, with family values, morals, and ethics until they were of school age.

For the first five to six years of our child's life, I was moderately content. Arguments, though quite severe, were not overly frequent. But they were always swept under the rug as the preference to address problems was simply not to. With a spouse who worked away from home three out of four weeks, I was the primary caregiver and life always goes on, so I went back to pretending to be happy, all the while not feeling valued, respected, or heard. As our child got older, more and more cracks in the marriage and family appeared, and as I studied them, and communicated what I thought and needed, I was always left back at working on myself and my part in those cracks, waiting for validation and wondering if efforts would ever be reciprocated.

Every once in a while when I recount something and a little regret pops up, I take a quick moment to acknowledge that feeling, then I force myself to speak a different truth about it, from "I didn't act, shame on me" to "I didn't act, because I didn't know how to yet." Going through a narcissistic abuse cycle takes a heavy mental and emotional toll on a person, and the journey through it has taught me to be more compassionate because more general kindness and compassion in today's world goes a really long way, as would a few other values and morals we seem to have lost sight of, integrity being another main one, and honesty, hard work, loyalty . . . but I digress. It is so easy to point fingers and judge, but it's much harder to turn that finger inward and make the same statement. Accountability and responsibility are two very important truths we all share. I try very hard now to live in the moment. Another lesson I've learned is to live presently and authentically and with integrity in all that I do; I am accountable and responsible for myself and my actions. This is how I point the finger at myself and live happily knowing I can be the best version of me. A good woman, mother, daughter, sister, friend, lover, and community member. I now know it is the healthy way to live; it is the only way to truly live and enjoy a happy, fulfilled life.

I fought and grew, failed, learned, and tried again until I found self-worth and awareness and self-love and self-respect for myself.

As it turns out, what I then thought was love was blind infatuation with the potential I saw in this person. But because change is hard and scary, most people choose to either not try or turn a blind eye to it. Stagnant people cannot flourish. I jumped too quickly into the relationship and became immersed in all that upset myself, in emotional, mental, verbal, and financial manipulation and control, and I stayed there for nearly fifteen years while I struggled, churned, and almost broke. But I fought and grew, failed, learned, and tried again until I found self-worth and awareness and self-love and self-respect for myself. I finally recognized that my values and priorities were different from his, and therefore, we were doomed.

Because we had a small child at that point, and I had no plan and still hoped that there was a light at the end of the tunnel, I thought the right thing to do was try to make it work while looking for a way to gain back my financial freedom and independence in case I needed to make the hard choice to be on my own again. I could make some more compromises to do that, couldn't I? Except I was the one that had done all the compromising and changing, to the point where I didn't recognize myself.

When we first met, there was boasting about my career choice. But after years of feeling devalued and criticized over it, I was emotionally worn down enough to give in to the persistence and change to a career that better fit someone else's value system. I wish I had listened to my body because it acknowledged what my mind could not, long before I understood it. During that career-change time especially, and also for the last five-ish years of the marriage, I was having a terrible time with gastroesophageal reflux disease (GERD) and indigestion, or so I thought. I would wake up from a dead sleep, usually at four or five a.m., and I would vomit stomach acid or retch stomach bile for what could be for hours on some mornings. Usually, I could get it under control by mid-morning, but I still steered clear of highly acidic foods, heavy spice, coffee, alcohol, etc., and I even started a medication for GERD. The part I find interesting now is that the trouble with indigestion finally stopped the day I left the marriage.

My own body had been reacting to the intensely stressful, unhealthy relationship and knew what was wrong all along. It wasn't a career change, although that didn't help. It worsened in that period because it wasn't something I wanted to do for myself and had said to friends and family at the time that I made the decision that I felt pressure to provide a better wage and pension for family security, again not aligning with my own values but repeating what I had heard over and over again. This was also the time that my spouse's second parent became terminally ill with cancer, and during this time, I learned many things about myself, the relationship, and the cycle we were in. My mind started opening to what my body had been screaming at me the whole time.

My mind started opening when my mother-in-law began releasing her life's trauma, and that's when I realized the full extent of the cycle I had been trying to survive in for so many years. I believe the cancer in her body manifested because she kept the pent-up years of emotional and mental abuse she had suffered in her own childhood inside her as well as her two marriages, because as everyone who knew her would say, she had hardly ever been physically sick or ill a day in her life. This beautiful, vibrant, lovely woman somehow had a body riddled with tumours at her life's end, the pain and anger radiating from within her. Toward the end, I never knew what state she was going to be in. I remember this one time being extremely worried, anxious, and scared when I brought our young child home from school that she might be drunk, as was the habit then, and verbally abusive while we tried to get homework and chores done. I kept reminding myself this was not the mother-in-law I loved; this woman was eaten away with cancer and anger, so couldn't I find it in myself to show her grace?! I tried and tried, until one day for no reason, she hit our child, and I had to call my spouse and tell him it was his mother leaving or his family. She was trying to make peace with herself I believe, but the trauma was so toxic at that point that it was all she could do to get it out of her, regardless of how and who it affected.

Days before she died, I had a chance to share my observations of her life situation with her. Alone together in her palliative care room, we talked briefly about her trauma and about how letting it go and understanding her own role in the progression of it up until that point was to ignore it or blame others, but only in accepting accountability for the decisions she made and how they got her to the point she was at would she find relief or peace. I told her that I held no anger toward her regardless of the past and that I loved and accepted her for her inner beauty, her flaws, and her weaknesses. We cried and touched arms briefly because she was too frail to hug, then talked about the weather and its seasonal changes. She smiled at me when I told her from the doorway that I'd see her soon, and she replied as she had when we'd first met, "You are so special." That was the last time I saw her alive. I grieved hard at her wake, where I was shunned by some of my in-laws for my lack of a role in the preparation of it. I bit my tongue that I had been the one truest by her side, through her darkest days at the end.

I celebrated her life in my own way by getting together with some friends who either knew her or had respect for her, by carrying a piece of her art and a prayer to the top of Pincushion Peak, a scenic Okanagan mountain hike, and by having a good cry and releasing a balloon filled with love and my prayer to her. I've felt peaceful with her since that day. I realized I had to make changes and I had to be honest with myself and set the right example for our child. I simply wasn't being my genuine self anymore and hadn't been in some time. I also didn't want to end up like that poor soul, broken and tortured, feeling angry, confused, and mostly alone at the end of her journey.

So, how did I get here, to the messiest situation I've ever been in in my life? Accountability and responsibility for myself is how. All the past happened, but what can I control and do about it now? Well, self-care is huge. Sleep, a good diet, and exercise are not enough. Emotional and mental self-care, keeping in a good headspace, staying organized, and functioning in a balanced way throughout the day are important. Also practicing breathing exercises daily. I know, right? Breathing! But yes, deep regular breaths, especially as soon as I feel anxiety, because I didn't realize it before but I'd actually stop breathing or take very shallow slow breaths. It's amazing how much easier it is to think after your brain gets oxygen. I've finally learned to control my fight-or-flight instincts, and I live mindfully in the present. Big lesson learned there. My dogs, who never waiver in unconditional love, help me do this—stay grounded in the present day, be outside, and actively live our best lives. They are and always have been my emotional support, and I'm proud of that and them. It is a healthy way to cope with the difficulties life can throw at you. Nature rejuvenates me and makes me really feel alive. In our big houses in congested cities, working and surviving day to day, we tend to forget what connected living really is.

In our big houses in congested cities, working and surviving day to day, we tend to forget what connected living really is.

The support of friends I trust is priceless, people who help me keep my core values in sight and motivate and inspire me to reach toward and achieve them. This has been a big learning lesson for me; I didn't have much of a network of "true to the core" friends before this because some of the people were not matching my values and so were unable to support me the way I needed. Now, I've stopped putting energy into friendships that are stagnant and/or challenging and have made the necessary changes by tightening my ring of trust. The backing from my trusted tribe has been phenomenal, and my family, especially, has been everything. I've had non-stop support and no judgment about my choice to finally change my life for the better, only love and forward thinking since I walked out of my marriage of nearly fifteen years. My parents, who are going through the most difficult life stage, two souls about to separate, have been my strongest well of strength. My focus for the coming months is their comfort, happiness, and quality of life as my father leaves this one. It's my turn to be the rock, which means staying focused on my health while another part of my family and life reorganizes.

As I find myself a single mother now, facing this crazy world and rebuilding my life and eventually a home in it again, I realize how culturally and generationally smart it is for primary family units to stay together, if they can. Moving into the future, my primary goal is to buy property that will sustain me, my child, my elderly mother, and my younger brother. With my brother and me carrying the burden of a large mortgage, it will allow my mother the time and ability to enjoy her golden years, and her grandchild. In today's world, communities are changing, revolving around the priorities of convenience, consumerism, and pandemic life, which is not always for the best. Community breakdowns are happening, and familial social networks are falling apart. This, to me, shows an extreme need now more than ever for strong communication and healthier family units and community rebuilding.

It also makes me wonder . . . Why are so many of we women left questioning our happiness, values, and sanity at this point? I somewhat believe it is because we are expected to be perfect mothers, perfect financial partners, perfect home keepers, perfect lovers, perfect friends . . . perfect. And somewhat because, in our hearts, our values and needs as human beings are not being met, so we need to align better with those values and the people who represent them. Friends, and especially family, are the people who should lift you up, and help you rise to the challenge of becoming the best person you can be. A person with no character, who holds your value from the past and is okay with lack of growth, is a stagnant person. They are not a person who can help themselves, let alone you. Let them go. Love yourself. Before you can love anyone else. A major lesson I wished I had learned earlier in life.

Two influences in my life, in particular, helped me learn this lesson. My mama, a strong woman of integrity and character, grew up surrounded by trauma and still chose to break her cycles and now helps others break theirs. And she managed to raise two accountable people while doing it. She's my rock and my guiding light because we all have light and dark within us. The other huge influence was my mother-in-law, RIP, a woman who, while broken in her trauma, still managed to shine a beautiful inner light and see light in others. She wasn't able to break her cycles and made worse choices as her life went on, but in doing so, provided me with learning and the opportunity to break my cycle, and at the end of hers, we found each other again. These two women, who I greatly love and respect, helped me navigate dark waters by learning to love their light and dark, something that forced me to see my own light and dark and start learning to love myself as well as feel compassion for and respect myself.

What I am facing right now is most difficult. I have had to realize and let go of the fact that I cannot control others' actions and decisions, I can only control my own. Finally finding the courage and strength to exit an unhappy, unhealthy marriage has forced me to set healthy boundaries for our child as well. Thus, I am now waiting for the time when we will reconnect. They are their own person, making their own choices, and this time we are apart now will be something for them to reflect on when they are older. For now, I communicate my love for them every day and wait. It has torn my heart in half, but I am slowly finding that time and acceptance of my decision to make the necessary changes for us both to have better lives meant this reset of our relationship was bound to happen eventually. My love for my work in education and the desire to create a new type of support centre for community health and education is what I focus on. I'm slowly upgrading my education to receive my Master's of ECE, not because I need it to open a centre, but because I believe it is relevant to prove the extent of the type of care I want to provide there. My appreciated presence back in the field was the pull I needed to get back on track doing what I love, and I am pretty good at, if I do say so myself. Knowing how to accept and be compassionate and respectful of your own abilities, strengths, and weaknesses is another valued lesson.

The peak of my self-care and accountability and responsibility as a good human and good family and community member is to establish, build, and live in the family-sustaining homestead and natural health and education centre that I have been dreaming about creating. Everything about this goal and idea is cultivated by and caters to my core values and therefore strengths. It encompasses not only my personal values and beliefs but that of my family's as well. It portrays the legacy that I challenge to others: kindness, compassion, integrity, respect, hard work, and education. My future looks bright. I'm working for an organization that fits my life goals, and it's helping me pay for upgrading to get to my best work-oriented self. Using that strategy, I am sure an opportunity to achieve my goal will come about: a "natural learning landscape" for children and animals to be safe and nurtured and to experience what real living should be like. It doesn't have to just be a dream.

My story ends with the challenge of me waiting, which is something I have never been good at, another lesson learned, especially once I've identified what it is I want. I am only in control of myself, and I will sit back and wait and watch and love and support my child from a distance, through their educational community and through technology. I know it's going to get worse before it gets better, but I am strong enough to face it now that I am re-aligned with my values. I'm waiting to receive and learn more life lessons through the next year or so, lessons of self-imposed singledom and personal journey. Although I started leaving emotionally and grieving my previous relationship before I actually ended it, I have done extensive self-perception checking and personal growth through that time. I'm now enjoying slowly finding my personal power again, and I look forward to the growing challenges the universe will bestow on me in the next while.

My challenge to you is to get uncomfortable with yourself. Honestly check in with your values and see where your happiness then lies. If anything I've said has resonated with you, feel free to reach out. I am now putting much energy into listening to, validating, and advocating the real-life struggle we women face in today's world. There are too many "tear you down" people, and now more than ever, we need more "hold you to your highest ability" people, and I, like my tribe, strive to help you become one of them. The feelings of self-worth and appreciation I have gained from stepping out of my unaligned life and comfort zone into my valued core self and learning zone are immensely satisfying. It's going to be a wait. A long one. And I know there will be more tough times ahead, but I'm stronger now and getting stronger every day. I keep learning, growing, listening, and working toward my values and goal. I know what I want now, and nothing is going to stand in my way. I know that the choices I've made are hard, but they will be worth it in the end because I am my valued self and have learned my lessons and found my fire.

For my mama and my mother-in-law (RIP). You made me who I am today. I have much love and respect for you both. Halfway through my life cycle, I'm humbled to say I have finally found a tribe of trusted souls, strong and independent women with whom I share core values and raw emotions with, who sing and dance and laugh and cry with me because they want to see me rise out of the flames and burn my truth into the sky.

Thank you; you know who you are.

My Child,

Your whole life I have said you are smart and capable. You will never lose, you will either win or learn. I cannot be there for the rest of your life, but I will love you for all of mine.

Shae Lemire-Cochrane has lived in the Okanagan Valley all her life except for a stayover in Thompson Country. She shares her home with her two beloved boxers, who are exceptionally spoiled. Before trying her hand at writing, Shae worked as an educator and community healthcare aide. Her passions include self-directed learning, helping people, dogs, music, networking and building community, homesteading, entertaining, gardening, and relaxing by a fire or a lake. She has one sibling and one child, and she is interested in leaving behind a legacy of integrity, kindness, compassion, and empowerment.

Chapter Nine

From the Ashes

Kate Ikert

I'm not like everyone else.

I am different.

I feel like a fish out of water most of the time.

I am a projector in human design and a profile 6/2. A non-energy type that wants to guide people, take naps, and work maybe three hours a day max. As a profile 6/2, I am the role model and the hermit.

I've had quite the life so far, but before we get into it, I need to give you a brief human design lesson.

Human design is your unique energy blueprint. It's based on the time and place of your birth. It is a combination of Chinese I'ching, Western and Eastern astrology, and the Judaic kabbalah. I thought it was pretty "out there" until I learned more about myself, and I've never felt more seen in my life.

The reason I teach through the lens of human design is because it is so profound. It's the operator's manual you didn't know you needed.

As a profile 6, I show up in the first thirty-ish years of my life like a profile 3—the experimenter. I like to call it the professional pivoter. Now that I am in my mid-thirties, I am shifting into the role model. I am here to share the lessons I have learned from being the experimenter. The timing of this book couldn't be more fitting. I am here to share my story with you in hopes that you see yourself in some of it. To maybe see how you don't fit in a box either. I know for me that boxes and labels feel safe, but they can also confine someone.

As I sit here writing this at the crack of dawn listening to Marianas Trench on repeat, coffee in hand, and not a single person awake but me, I'm basking in the alone time. It's where I thrive. Being alone feels good, safe, easy, and expected. Is it lonely sometimes? Yes, that's also why I hang out with other projectors because they just get it.

I can't do small talk; it drains me. I don't do group settings unless I am the leader. I really thrive 1:1. Having three kids is exhausting, and I am a sponge for everyone else's "sloppy seconds" energy. The gross, negative stuff that no one else wants.

I am a mom of three living on a grain farm in southeast Saskatchewan with my husband, Bryan, and three dogs. I am a former registered nurse and now multi-passionate entrepreneur running multiple businesses and currently enrolled in Shaman school. I am an intuitive, psychic medium, human design expert, coach, spiritual mentor, and guide. I have a love of music and a desire to learn how to DJ and a love of pottery with a slight obsession with mugs. As you can see, I don't fit in a box. I am a paradox through and through.

It's an interesting thing when telling your story. There doesn't seem to be any way to start. So, I'm just going to dive in because that's my style. No small talk.

My dad was an abusive alcoholic.

I was only eight when my sister called the police to have him arrested. My sisters are seven and ten years older than I am, so when he was gone, it was just my mom and me left together.

It wasn't until I was twelve that I finally understood what he did. It's interesting looking back now, though. I remember thinking that I had to avoid seeing him to make everyone else happy. That if I shared in the mutual hatred of him, I would somehow feel more included in my family.

The truth is, they had a whole life before I came along. I never really felt accepted, and this is something I still struggle with today. I would rather be alone then around people that make me feel alone. Isolated in a room with others I think is the hardest. To never really be seen.

The truth is, when my dad was gone, I didn't just lose him, I lost my entire family. My oldest sister went to college, my middle sister coped in her own way and hung out with friends and was rarely ever home, and my mom did the best she could given the circumstances while working in the city for most of the day. I was alone a lot of the time, and it became what I know and what's safe.

I knew they would be there at the drop of a hat for me if I needed them, but I have limited memories of us as a family. If there is anything that still hurts, it is that.

I spent a good portion of my childhood escaping to my friend Lynda's house. They were family friends for as long as I could remember. I would go to her house after school when things got really bad with my dad, and I would stay there. Lynda felt like family. Funny enough, she just joined me as a business partner and that thirty-year friendship has grown into so much more. She's my best friend and the person that has been my rock through all of it.

I remember one day she came over to my house and I could hear my dad screaming in the kitchen. We stayed in the bedroom knowing that it was the safest option. We kept playing, and I knew she was always looking out for me. She was there in a way that, looking back now, I didn't know a twelve-year-old could be.

Lynda's dad died suddenly five years ago, and it shook me to my core. It was very confusing at the time. I ended up talking to a counsellor because I couldn't process the grief, and they gave me the permission I needed to grieve. He had been the only father figure I had in my life. He had been my water polo coach and the one who picked me up from the side of a toilet after too many Smirnoff coolers around their bonfire as a teenager. He was a wonderful man, and as I write this, I'm brought to tears and feel gratitude for the wonderful impact he had on my life.

Family doesn't have to be blood. It doesn't have to look how you think it will.

I continued to have a complicated relationship with my own father, and his sudden passing in 2008 was confusing for me. I was in nursing school at the time and wasn't sure how to process this news. Classmates reached out to me saying they were sorry, and I kept saying it was okay. Grief is interesting—it isn't black or white. It didn't make sense, and I didn't know how to grieve something I had already lost. At the time of his passing, I was involved in a group project and was being graded through peer reviews. I almost didn't pass because I was given a low grade for lack of participation. I was processing the death of my dad, telling everyone I was fine, and I was being taken at my word. But I was obviously not fine. This is also why I needed the permission to grieve when my friend's dad died because it was messy, complicated, and didn't make sense.

It wasn't until October 31, 2020, when I forgave my dad. I set his picture, along with my grandma and grandpa-in-law's on an altar.

It was in that moment that I let my intuition guide me, and I received the message that he loved me very much, but his demons kept him from being able to show that to me. It was never a lack of love for me but, in fact, a lack of self-love that kept him in the shame-guilt spiral, never fully allowing himself to be the father we needed. I forgave him at that moment and let him go. I remember feeling this weight lift off my shoulders, and I could hear him say thank you. I don't remember much of my dad. I actually don't have any happy memories with him, but I do hope and pray that no matter where he is, he's at peace.

It's really interesting as I reflect on what I had been through up until this point. After my dad passed away, I felt like I never really did grieve him properly or process his death when it happened. I carried it in my body for longer than I realized, and the unprocessed trauma had a hold on me that I wasn't aware of.

I started having chest pain. I was in nursing school when it first happened, and the nurse at the college gave me an antacid, diagnosing me with heartburn. I've had heartburn and knew this wasn't heartburn. It felt like knives were stabbing me in my throat. Even as I write these words, I can feel them again. This went on for months. I took antacids to "help," but they never did. I was taking Tylenol and Advil to manage the pain, which quickly turned into Tylenol 3s, which worked until they didn't.

It was March 2007 when the pain landed me in the emergency room. I remember my now-husband driving me to the hospital so scared. I was in such a daze. I think I blacked out from the pain. It felt exactly like chest pains I used to have as a kid, something I hadn't remembered up until this point.

I remember lying on my bed in my childhood home. My comforter was pastel pink fleece on one side with multi-coloured pastel hearts on the other. The room was spinning. Have you ever swallowed a chip or cracker the wrong way and you can feel it go all the way down? That's what it felt like, except I hadn't been eating anything. I lay on my bed and allowed it to pass. I guess that was my first episode. I was nine at the time.

At the hospital, I received heavier doses of painkillers, and this continued on for a number of months with a vague diagnosis of esophageal spasms.

Fast-forward to 2010 when we got married in October and moved to Saskatchewan two months later, 1,000 kilometres from everyone and everything I had ever known, two days after finishing my final practicum in nursing. We had made the decision to move to Saskatchewan, as there were limited nursing jobs at the time and the state of the healthcare system in Alberta appeared to be worsening. My husband wanted to continue the family farm, and I had a job lined up with the hospital. We weren't in our current hometown for a month when the chest pains started again. I wasn't even working at the hospital yet, so my future co-workers already knew me as a patient. Not the first impression I wanted to make. The pain continued on for years. Still no answers as to why.

In December 2011, I got pregnant with our first baby. I was excited and nervous to see how things progressed with my chest pains while I was pregnant, and unfortunately, they continued. There were times when I required high doses of narcotics and was put on heavy medications during my pregnancy to manage the pain. My pregnancy was all-around healthy in most regards. My daughter was born in September 2012, and the cycle continued, except now, I had someone else to care for too.

I became pregnant with my second in February 2015. I had many more complications with this pregnancy. I had early contractions starting at twenty weeks, gained a massive amount of weight, and ended up being induced due to preeclampsia.

It was the end of November 2015 when I jumped on a scale. I had gained more than eighty pounds while pregnant. I was mortified. How did this happen? It wasn't just about the weight, I know we are beautiful at any size, but it wasn't about beauty. I wasn't healthy. I didn't sleep well (newborn or not). I didn't nourish my body, I rarely drank water, I wasn't physically active, and I wasn't taking care of myself. In January 2016, I started to slowly change that. I committed to taking a yoga class every week. Then, after two months, I added in something else. I slowly made small changes to my diet and continued moving my body in a way that felt good for me. I started feeling better, healthier, but the chest pains persisted.

June 2016, I was on the highest dose of narcotics I could be on without passing out. It was starting to get out of control, and I knew that, but I didn't know where to turn. I was going into the city for regular gastroscopies two to three times a year, where they would stretch out my esophagus and inject Botox to help with the pain. It only helped temporarily. I also tried a few alternative medicines such as acupuncture, but to no avail.

How long was I supposed to keep going like this? In and out of the hospital on high-dose narcotics with two kids at home? I was barely functioning. We were consulting with doctors in the States and in the process of consulting with the Mayo Clinic. The cost of all these things was starting to add up, including the time I had been off work and also the time my husband took. Something had to change.

My mom had connections with a doctor in Calgary for a fresh set of eyes and maybe a diagnosis that the other doctors who had been working so hard to help me were unable to find.

It was in summer 2016 when I finally had a consultation with this doctor. After running tests, he looked me in the face and said, "I am really sorry, my dear, but there is nothing physically wrong at this time. Is there anything else that's going on in your heart that might be bothering you?"

I broke down. It all came flooding in. Years of not speaking up, years of not asking for what I wanted or needed because those around me didn't have the ability to hold space for me in the way that I needed. For so long I had people appease me, rightfully so, but that doctor saw me in a way that I have never been seen. It was a moment of empowerment. I remember thinking, *okay, if there isn't anything physically wrong with me, then it is up to me to get better. I am in control of what happens now.* I can't even explain it. It's like something that had been dormant was suddenly activated.

I was on thirteen different medications at the time, including heart medications, muscle relaxants, medication to combat the side effects of some of the medications I was on, and high-dose narcotics. More than any twenty-seven-year-old should be on. I thought this was going to be my life, but at that moment, that doctor gave me the permission I didn't know I needed to choose to start again, to rewrite my story, and to decide who it is I wanted to be going forward.

Was it all anxiety? Was it my body screaming at me to deal with the shit on my heart?

My intuition tells me yes, but what's funny is that I felt like I needed an explanation. Not for me, but for others. The truth is that I don't know what changed; it wasn't just one thing. I threw everything I could at it. At the end of the day, I do believe I made the choice that this wouldn't be my story anymore.

When I think back to my childhood, I realize that when I was sick, I received the love and compassion I was looking for. This is common. People identify as the victim, as the sick one, subconsciously wanting to stay sick because they get their deepest emotional needs met. I believe this was definitely a part of it.

At the end of the day, I do believe I made the choice that this wouldn't be my story anymore.

I still sometimes get tightness in my chest, but I approach it with love, compassion, and curiosity. As a projector, it now feels like my "check engine" light: a reminder to rest, sleep, and slow down. I ask myself the most important questions:

Have I had enough water?

Have I moved my body? (even just a five-minute walk or kitchen dance party).

Am I nourishing my body?

The hardest part looking back on my health journey has been the triggers. My two oldest are in grades one and four. My youngest, two, is further along developmentally than either their siblings were by this point, which breaks my heart because I can't help but think that their delays, the reason they struggle at school, their frustration, their inability to cope and focus is my fault. They struggle to learn, to read and write, and it is a daily reminder of what went on. I can't help but often wonder if I had just dealt with the shit on my heart, maybe none of this would have happened.

I wish someone would have helped me in the way I needed to be helped instead of my experiencing painful procedure after procedure. I wish that someone would have said to me, "Maybe there's more going on here." I also have gratitude for my journey. I truly believe that your mess becomes your message. Whenever I see someone who has fallen through the cracks of the system, it breaks my heart. I can't wait to be a resource to many. A medicine woman who can help people on a deeper level—to help not only survive, but to thrive as well.

I now know I'm right where I am meant to be, doing the work I feel pulled to do. Helping others heal in such a deep and profound way. As a nurse, the favourite part of my job was maternity and palliative care. Bearing witness and being the person that is present when life enters and leaves this world is one of the most powerful experiences of my life. As a shaman, I get to do that work again. I can be there when these amazing souls enter and leave this world. I wasn't meant to be a nurse, and I am right where I am meant to be.

I didn't want to share this part of my story. It's dark and shameful, but I do feel it is necessary.

I mostly don't want to hurt those that I love who see me a certain way, and I fear that my kids will get caught up in it. I also remember the words of the deeply inspiring Brené Brown: "Write what it is you need to hear." This is what I needed to hear.

Your actions don't define you.

In spring 2018, I had an affair. It's funny because it's not what one would think. It was deeply unfulfilling, mostly an emotional connection that I was looking for.

I now know I was trying to get my needs met. My seven-year-old self was longing for connection. To be seen, heard, held. I wish I could go back to that 2018 version of myself and give her so much love. She was so alone, lost, confused, scared, sad. Doing the best she could and trying so hard to do what she needed to do to be okay. As weird as it sounds, I am so grateful it happened. I'm not happy that I hurt my husband, but here's the great thing about rock bottom—it gives you a place to jump off of.

I've realized that mistakes I have made, or things I have done, do not have to define me. That I can heal and forgive myself for the things I feel shame around and that if I do the work, my past doesn't have to be my future. That those things aren't my identity going forward.

Fuck societal standards. People cheat all the time, and I am not going to let it mean what people make it mean. It's not some scandalous event. It's a hurt person trying to be okay. Hurt people, hurt people. It's the wounded inner child trying to get their needs met. When I could look at it from such a logical perspective, it was then that I could start healing from it. I learned how to communicate with my spouse and for us to see each other and heal the parts of ourselves that didn't get what we needed as children.

You see, I had responsibility thrust upon me when I was eight when my dad left and it was essentially just me and my mom. When my husband and I moved to the farm and he left frequently, I felt abandoned and responsible for everything. It was like being eight all over again. Escaping reality and not facing the responsibility was a way to cope. Was it healthy? Hell no, but I can't change it, I can only learn from it.

There are people that are going to share this news like juicy gossip. Maybe they already have. We live in a small town, and that's the reality sometimes, but I didn't share this part of my story for them. I share this piece of my journey not for me, but for the 2018 version of myself that needed to not feel so alone in what had happened and for the person who needs to not feel alone right now.

My worth isn't based on how other people view me. That isn't my truth. Love is my truth. I am not my mistakes or circumstances. Some hard shit has happened in my life, but it doesn't define me. It's there to show me where the growth needs to happen. Where the stories that have been on repeat that no longer serve me need to be rewritten.

It wasn't just one thing that forced me into communication with someone else, and just like how it took thousands of years of water running through the Grand Canyon to create the spectacular structure we know today, so is what happened here.

It was consistency over time. Consistent miscommunication, consistent lack of awareness, consistent trying to meet our own love languages and not each other's, consistent avoidance of the work we both needed to do, consistent coping with unhealthy distractions such as drinking, time with others that would trigger us, health issues, work, Netflix, social media, etc.

This event forced both of us to look in the mirror we had been avoiding.

It was a beautiful, messy, and deeply healing experience for us both. To finally be seen for who we truly are, what we truly need, then asking for our needs to be met. To communicate in an effective manner with each other and not just how we had seen generational communicative patterns play out. Just because that's the norm doesn't mean it's okay.

Rewriting old patterns, healing generational trauma, and redefining yourself over and over again is fucking hard work. We continue to work on our marriage every day, and interestingly enough, that looks like doing the individual work. We can't be there for each other if we aren't there for ourselves. It's not our job to make each other happy but to make ourselves happy, and in doing that, we will have the deeply fulfilling relationship we both want.

There are people lucky enough in this world to have never truly suffered. They have never lost a loved one, they have never hit rock bottom, they have never been through the hard shit. But there is nothing more powerful than being forged in the fire and rising like a Phoenix from the ashes. It has completely moulded me into who it is that I am today.

I am grateful for every single lesson and opportunity to grow through what I have and am going through.

If you can't even see the forest through the trees, I want you to know this: Your mess can become your message. Your test can be your testimony. I believe that God, the Universe, whatever speaks to you, doesn't give you more than you can handle. I know it can be heavy and hard, and not every moment can be good, but there is good in every moment.

Keep going, don't quit, and don't let your story define you. You get to rewrite your story over and over again. It's not too late. You don't have to be a victim of your circumstances. It doesn't have to take you out. You can rise. Like that Phoenix from the ashes. Let that fire forge and mould you into who you truly are.

The world needs your light. Please don't dim it. It's not going to look like everyone else's, and that's the point! You are a once-in-a-lifetime cosmic event. Do you even know what it took for you to get here? The actual odds of you being here at this moment, picked from the millions of sperm and thousands of eggs, are in the trillions. You are not here by accident.

As I reflect on everything I have been through in my life, I realize it was all happening for me. I thought there was something wrong with me, but what I now realize is that life is a journey of learning and unlearning. Healing and growing. Expansion and deeper self-compassion. As you navigate your own journey, I hope you can find comfort in this quote by Rumi the same way I did.

"The wound is the place where the light can enter."

Let it be your guidepost; let it be your reminder. Your past does not define you.

To Bryan. For all the growth, learning, redefining, and grace.

To Ada, Reece, and Wilder. My greatest growth journey and opportunity to break down ancestral trauma so that you don't have to.

To Paige. I would not be where I am today without you in my life, and I am forever grateful to you and your wisdom.

To my team. I love you so much!

To Lynda. For being there when it really matters!

To my mom for doing the best she could and being brave when it mattered most.

To my sisters for looking out for me and always wanting what is best for me.

To everyone who has been there along the way and met me with the deepest compassion, thank you.

Kate Ikert is a registered nurse by trade who retired in August 2020 after ten years. She started her successful business with Arbonne in May 2019, and she is now in the top 8 percent of the company. Kate pivoted into what she is currently doing today and is running a successful online coaching business where she helps female entrepreneurs increase their income and impact. She is an intuitive, psychic medium, human design expert, coach, spiritual mentor, and guide. Kate is a Level II Certified Reiki Practitioner and is currently enrolled in Shaman school which she is expected to complete Summer 2023.

Originally from High River, Alberta, Kate currently resides on a farm in southeast Saskatchewan with her husband, Bryan, three children, Ada (9), Reece (6), and Wilder (2), and their three dogs, Duke, Joey, and Mater.

Kate is passionate about helping other women redefine what it means to be a Canadian woman, to challenge the societal expectations of what it looks like to be a mom and wife.

"Here to help women burst out of the box even though it's uncomfortable."

Chapter Ten

A Different Kind of Fairy Tale

Sky Edwards

I was the girl who grew up believing in fairy tales. My whole life I dreamed of that perfect, effortless love story, and I really thought that would be my experience in life. I was impatient when it came to finding love, getting married, and living my happily ever after. My imagination always jumping ahead of where my reality was, making me oblivious to what was actually happening around me at times. So much so that I thought my high school sweetheart would be it for me, only to be crushed when I found myself heartbroken shortly after throwing my all into the relationship. Looking back, moving out at eighteen, in together at nineteen, and trying to plan forever freshly out of high school without even knowing who I was or what I wanted out of life probably wasn't my best life plan. I wish I knew then what I know now, but I was young and on a mission, so, when that relationship ended, I moved back home and started the search for my next love story.

It didn't take me long to jump into the very next relationship that became available to me. I was a young woman who was being swept off her feet by an older high school crush who knew who insignificant little me was after all, and it sounded like the fairy tale beginning of my forever love story. The beginning was a whirlwind of emotions and a whole lot of red flags I was too naive to see and gladly ignored because I had convinced myself that this was it. How could such an intense relationship not be what every girl dreamed of? The fights, the passion, the love, the tears, the highs and lows—it was everything every chick flick and romance novel I obsessed over depicted, and it was manifesting itself right in front of me. I felt like the luckiest girl in the world.

A year into the relationship things were still very much intense, and as time went on, I did have moments when I questioned whether it was the right relationship for me. Somehow, I continued to find reasons to keep dismissing those feelings, and shortly after found myself pregnant, engaged, living together, and planning for a baby and a wedding. Everything I had dreamed of was working itself out by the time I turned twenty-one, only this dream was starting to look and feel like one a part of me wanted to wake up from.

Life as a young mom took a huge toll on me and my relationship. There were so many times I wasn't sure I would make it down that aisle. There were so many times that timeouts were called on our relationship because there were a lot more lows than highs. There was a lot of fighting within the relationship and for the relationship because regardless of how hard it all was, I wanted it to work. This tiny family was my whole world now, but I was learning in a short amount of time that love wasn't as easy as it had been made out to be. I was learning that you had to work for it, sacrifice for it, fight for it, and cherish it. So, that's what I did. We said our I do's, and I had my happily ever after, only I had come to realize that that's not how it works. There is no happily ever after, but I was married and that was a commitment I would keep, no matter what. I took my vows to heart, and I believed that marriage was forever. So, our life together as husband and wife began. The intensity between us never faded. There was a lot of passion and love but also a lot of hurt and unmet expectations that slowly piled their way up. I felt myself shrinking to try and avoid confrontation. It felt easier to just be small than to stand up for myself and create waves. Easier to stay silent and try to fill the role of happy wife than speak up or ask for help.

I thought I had to do whatever it took to keep us all together, even if it meant losing myself in the process. I promised "until death do us part," after all. I promised to stay for the good and bad, so I slowly became everything I needed to be to make it work. Quiet, small, insignificant. I gave up who I was and who I wanted to be because I needed to be what I believed my husband wanted me to be. I wanted to make him happy, and I didn't want to fail as his wife.

I was told to be softer, more feminine, to make him feel needed, to be grateful that he still wanted me. I slowly gave pieces of myself away—chipped away so slowly and gradually over time that I hadn't noticed just how much I gave up. I was slowly becoming someone I no longer recognized. I felt like a shell of a human being, lifeless and dull, navigating the world around me. When I was out in the world, I had this wall of happiness that I tried to keep up. I needed people to believe I was happy and that everything was okay. I had worked so hard and given up so much of myself, my dreams, my wants and needs to make this work, and I needed it to work. But that wall started to crumble, and no matter how hard I tried to keep it together, I couldn't. Piece by piece, the parts of our marriage I tried to hide found their way into the light. Those closest to me started to see just how broken I was. I was falling apart, and I couldn't hide how bad it had gotten, but I wasn't ready to give up or call it. I couldn't afford to fail at this because this is what I wanted. This was the dream, after all.

My little girl was the one who changed everything. As she got older, she started to see through that poorly structured wall, and I knew that by continuing down this road, I wasn't just losing myself, I was failing her. She deserved so much more from me as a mother. She deserved someone and something to look up to, and I wasn't being who she needed me to be. This little girl who was so full of love, life, and fire was feeling the turmoil I was in. She could feel me breaking, and I couldn't keep using her as the person who was holding me together. I couldn't keep being this version of myself, and I couldn't keep living this life while knowing that she was watching and soaking it all in. I couldn't let this be what her normal was. I couldn't let this be her life one day. Her reference of love, life, marriage, and happiness. This couldn't be it for her.

The problem was that I didn't believe in divorce. It was ingrained in me that divorce was bad. That it was the easy way out and that it made one a failure. A failure at love. A failure at marriage. A failure as a woman. A failure to my daughter. All the things you don't want to fail at, and here I was, making this decision because I didn't have any other one to make. The shame as I came to terms with what I had to do weighed heavy on me because I desperately wanted another option, but it was clear there wasn't one.

Making the decision to separate was one of the hardest decisions I had made up to that point in my life. I was made to feel guilty, I felt ashamed, and I felt unsupported through most of the process. In my heart I knew it was the right decision, but the shame inside me, along with the shame others put on me, made me question whether I was just being selfish. Honestly, there were moments when I didn't think I'd be able to go through with it. I wondered if I deserved to be happy because I was breaking up my family. I had people ask me if I would change my mind or regret making this decision. Honestly, going through the process of ending a marriage is long and tedious, and I kind of hoped that along the way something would change and I wouldn't have to go through with it. That hopeless romantic in me hoped for a miracle, but it was made very clear that this wasn't a fairy tale and that there would be no happy ending here. So, I continued the process.

I felt like people couldn't see the weight I was carrying in making this decision. It wasn't one I was making to be cruel. It was one I was making to survive, to breathe, to live, because I wasn't doing any of those things anymore. I was simply existing even though I wasn't sure I even wanted to. The heaviness of trying to make this relationship work when it was never meant to was nothing less than tragic. The soul-crushing reality that not all love stories are fairy tales, and the idea that some are full-blown horrors and tragedies, was gut-wrenching. I was devastated and heartbroken, and there were moments I didn't think I could survive it. I acted out and lashed out and did things I wish I could take back because my heart was being ripped from my chest in the process. Everything I had built, everything I had planned, everything I had wanted with this person was ending, and in the process, I didn't just lose a husband, I lost everything I thought I wanted. We became strangers overnight, and all the I love yous turned into I hate yous in the blink of an eye. It made me question whether love really existed at all.

So, there I was alone, lost and broken. Feeling helpless and turning to those I thought cared about me only to find myself blindsided. Sides were chosen, and, of course, my side was empty. This only solidified the idea of how unworthy I was of love. Instead of friends and a support system, I had an audience waiting, watching, and hoping to see me fail, to see me miserable. And they added to the pain and guilt that already weighed heavy on me. They reminded me that this decision would have consequences even I couldn't have fathomed. I guess one of the worst parts about marrying and divorcing the popular guy in town is everyone wanted a piece of the action. A front-row seat to the drama. They wanted to know the inside scoop, even if it was all one-sided. Even if there wasn't much of any truth to it at all.

The weeks and months to follow were nothing short of a nightmare. All the things I had prepared myself for didn't even begin to cover how my life would begin to unfold. I was at a job surrounded by his friends. Everywhere I turned in our small town, they were there. Every look, every word, every step or action had repercussions. Every breath I took felt heavy, and I realized that even though I was no longer in this relationship, I wasn't free from it either. Having a daughter together reminded me that I never would be, but I hadn't expected it to feel like a prison. I wasn't prepared to feel so exposed. Every time I let loose or tried to find some type of normalcy as I moved through this new chapter I was stalked, filmed, blackmailed, or messaged. It's like no matter what I did, where I went, or who I was with, everyone was watching, and everyone was sharing and comparing intel.

I was being suffocated by my new reality, and instead of handling it well, I did the exact opposite. If everyone wanted to know what I was up to at all times, and wanted something to talk about, I would give that to them. So, I put myself on display. I made myself the messy bitch they seemed to long for, and I did it right in front of all of them. No more hiding. No more trying to live discreetly. No more giving a shit, because it wasn't working anyway. Somehow, I was the villain in this story, so I figured why not live up to that reputation? I already didn't know who I was, while everyone else thought they did, so why not give up more of myself to fit into this new role they believed I belonged in? I guess when you're already so lost, it becomes easier to lose yourself some more.

We talk about nature and nurture as if those are the only two things that play a role in who we become.

Drunken nights, bad decisions, countless hookups, hurtful words and lots of screaming, fighting and things I can't take back or even remember. All the reasons I left my marriage forgotten as I gave in to the hurt, rage, and brokenness. I left to find peace, only to create a lot more hell for myself and for those around me. I became the person I hated most in the process. A decision I had made out of love for my daughter became selfish and pathetic. I was spending less time with her; I was no example any little girl deserved, and I hated myself for that. I chose pettiness over the role of being a good mother, and the shame I felt was heavier than any shame I had about a failed marriage.

How does one lose themselves in such a profound way? It was a question I couldn't help but ask myself as I looked at who I had become. I didn't recognize her. I didn't love her. I didn't even understand her anymore, and I didn't know what to do about that. I realized that in my current state, I wasn't worthy of love, at least not the kind of love I wanted for myself. For the first time in a long time, I felt the weight of those words in a very different way. Instead of someone using them as a weapon against me, I used them as a wake-up call. A reality check. A moment of "What the fuck are you doing with your life?" Here I was, this young twenty-three-year-old mom to this beautiful little girl who loved me even at my worst, and I knew in that moment that I found myself being done yet again with being this version of myself. She deserved so much more from me, and if I wanted to deserve more and believe that I was worthy of more, then this reality had to end. This time there was no one to blame but me, as I had chosen this path. One that wasn't worthy of my daughter.

It was time I found the root of the problem and stopped placing the blame on people who let me down, the relationships that didn't work out, and the people who just couldn't love me right. It was time I focused on ME and not only on how I ended up there, but also how I would move forward. I had to do more than just leave a relationship or a marriage, I had to decide that every choice I made going forward would be one of purpose!

Growing up, I never thought much about who I was and how I became that person, I always just was that person, forever growing and changing as my circumstances changed. I thought that's just what happened and how it worked. You grew up and became who you were meant to be. That logic no longer made sense to me because I wasn't who I used to be or who I thought I would be. I definitely wasn't even close to the kind of person I wanted to be. It wasn't until I turned inward and started reading and listening to self-development and discovery books that I really started to realize how much I didn't know and how misled I was with the information I was given and the lack of information I never received. I was always asked what I wanted to be when I was older, rarely if ever being asked who I wanted to be. I was asked a lot about what I was looking for in a partner, but I was never asked who I would need to be in order to be ready or worthy for that kind of partner, let alone who I would need to be to be okay with not having one.

I felt like I was given this false narrative of what love and life was and how it all worked, only to be blown away by the vast amount of information out there that was never-ending and beyond intriguing. I grew up believing I had to be this version of me without realizing the capacity I had as an individual to question, grow, and change in unlimited ways. We talk about nature and nurture as if those are the only two things that play a role in who we become. Those forces outside our control are the only things that shape us into the people we are going to be, without being taught that we can play a role and have so much control over that. That with the right tools and the right questions, we have the capacity to become someone else entirely. This awakening and information overwhelmed me and started me on a course in my life that I hadn't even known was an option. I no longer had to be who I thought I was. I no longer had to be who anyone else thought I was or who they assumed me to be, and I definitely didn't have to try and fit into some mould that I didn't create for myself.

This was an uncomfortable realization, as I knew that by becoming who I truly was and wanted to be, it would mean I would have to own up to the role I had played in my life and relationships up until this point. It meant that I would have to acknowledge that I didn't love myself right, and therefore, I couldn't show others how I wanted or expected to be loved. It also meant I had to accept that I didn't love right either. That my version of love was unhealthy and all-consuming and came with a long list of conditions—ones that were sometimes unfair, unattainable, or not communicated in the right way.

It also meant that everyone in my life would have to learn who I was all over again, just as I would. It meant letting go of all this stuff I was holding on to that wasn't making me or my life any better. It also meant having to be okay when others didn't understand my actions or decisions. I had to learn to respect people, even if it meant not aligning with them or their versions of right and wrong. I was finally in the driver's seat, blocking out all the noise of those who thought they knew better so that I could become my version of better.

I can't say that it was a smooth transition. I messed up. I reverted to old patterns. I questioned whether I was making the right decisions and sometimes second-guessed myself a whole heck of a lot. This was not a perfect journey, and I know now that I could have handled a lot of the change better than I did. I could have made better decisions. I could have been kinder to those who struggled with me changing. I could have had more patience and trust in the process. The thing about growth is it is never-ending, and we always see how we could have done better once we know better. But this process was a worthy one.

Small conscious decisions and changes. That is what I would focus on so that I could rebuild myself and my life. Instead of focusing on the mess and destruction of the past, I would focus on the now, the present, because that is how I would build my future. Every decision would be intentional going forward. I quit my job for one with hours that worked with me being a mom and with people who weren't in any way tied to the previous version of my life. I slowly cut ties with people who weren't good for me and started trusting my gut when it came to who I should allow to occupy time and space in my life. I spent more time getting to know my daughter and the amazing person she was and is. I started asking for help when I needed it. I started rebuilding relationships within my family. I stopped being petty and giving people things to talk about on purpose. I started saving money and making a plan to move out of this town that was holding me back in more ways than one. I slowly put small pieces of me and who I wanted to be back together, all while devouring information about self-development, and I gradually started becoming the me I deserved and the mother my daughter deserved.

Piece by piece, I found a little bit more of myself. I found that I had a lot to give and a whole hell of a lot to live for. I fell in love with myself and the person I was becoming and realized that was one of the most important relationships I had and would ever have going forward. I stopped looking for love, fulfillment, and worth from other people, and I started creating it for myself. I worked on building a life for me and my daughter in the midst of all the chaos and change happening in our lives. I wouldn't say things got easier throughout the divorce process, but I became more assured and confident in my actions and following through with the decisions I was making when it came to my life and my daughter's. I became extremely focused on trying to be better and to own the role I played in getting us here. I was focusing on the bigger picture, even when it was hard and pettiness wanted to find its way in. Every decision going forward was made out of love and respect for myself and the life I was creating. That is what kept me grounded and on the right path. This is how I continue to live my life, even to this day.

Ten years later and I'm still learning so much about myself. My whole world has changed in such a drastic way because of this one decision that was followed by countless more tiny decisions and some even bigger ones. When I look at my life, I am forever grateful for the lessons I learned through love and heartache. My divorce wasn't the end of my love story but the beginning of my true love story. The story where I learned how to love me, how to love others, and how to truly allow others to love me. Becoming a mother taught me what love really was, and now I am surrounded by it.

I know that divorce was the right decision for me. When I look at my oldest and see them watching me be loved in the right way, I know it within every fibre of my body. They will know what love is supposed to look and feel like because it's their reality now. They have a mom who actually loves and respects herself, who even if they don't realize it yet, is someone they can be proud of one day. They see me love fiercely in my marriage, with them, our family, their siblings, and in everything I do. This little person making me a mother was the beginning of me becoming the woman I am today. Those bright eyes that looked up at me as if I were their whole world, changed everything. In believing they deserved better, I learned that I did too, and now we are building that life day by day.

We only have this one life here on this earth and I remind myself of that often. I think choosing your path, choosing your happiness, and fighting for a better and truer version of yourself in this life is a worthy way to live. I think growing and expanding is what life is all about, and sometimes that means things don't work out the way you thought you wanted or needed them to. Sometimes we outgrow our current situations, and no amount of force will fix it. Sometimes things end, and in my experience, that isn't always a bad thing. My marriage ending didn't feel like a blessing but in looking back, it was the biggest gift I ever received. Without it, this life, this love, this family, and this version of me wouldn't exist and that would have been the real tragedy.

This chapter is dedicated to all the women who came before me, and all the women who will come after. It has taken so much to get to the point where we can not only share our stories but make the decisions in our lives to create them.

This chapter is for my oldest child, Charlye, who was, and still is, my "why" when I needed one the most, and to my other children, Rayen, Lennox, and Milo who continue to show me just how strong and capable I am as a woman and mother.

To my husband who has played a huge role in my growth and is my biggest cheerleader.

Thank you for the kind of love and patience every woman deserves.

Mom and Dad, thank you for giving me a safe place to land and re-find my footing.

I am beyond grateful for how my life has turned out and the woman I have and am still becoming.

Sky Edwards is a wife, mother, and woman who is passionate about inspiring other women to love themselves through every stage in life. She shares openly about her struggles with body image, divorce, pregnancy loss, mental health, motherhood, and her struggles to find herself along the way in hopes to normalize these conversations and give other women hope and encouragement in their journeys.

She has created an online community and following by showing up in all her messy chaos and chronically oversharing all over social media. In doing so, she has learned that there is a beautiful and powerful strength that happens when we learn to trust in ourselves and show up authentically.

She has expanded in the way she has been able to share and reach other women by beginning to speak at women's events online and hopefully in person in the future. She became a published author in *The Great Canadian Woman — She Is Strong and Free III*, which led her to becoming lead author in *She Is Full of Fire*.

Sky has big plans for the future, and with every new thing she has accomplished, she has gained more confidence in her ability to connect and help women, and her fire burns even brighter with every step forward.

Final Words

It took so much courage and fire from each author to share their stories in such a raw and powerful way. The goal was for each author to feel pride in their chapter, to stay true to themselves and their voice, and to realize just how far they have come, and for a lot of us, it was another step in our healing process. Throughout the process, we all had the desire to reach other women through our stories and to be a sense of hope and inspiration to each reader, knowing we needed and wanted that during these times in our own lives.

The beautiful and emotional work that comes from sharing pieces of ourselves with others is a worthy one, but not always an easy one. It involves becoming vulnerable, letting down our walls, and sharing our hearts with total strangers, all in hope that someone somewhere will feel seen and heard.

We hope that after reading our stories you feel less alone in all that you have, are, or will go through in this life. We hope you feel inspired, empowered, and seen. We hope you realize just how not alone you are, because that realization is priceless. We hope you know that the fire inside these women is also inside you.

I am beyond proud of these women for trusting themselves over and over again. For trusting in this process and for sharing without holding back. I'm proud that you have decided to pick up and read this book, giving these women's stories a place to land and hopefully inspiring you to one day share your own story and fire with those around you.

Endnotes

Chapter Two by Cayman Ferguson

A Farewell to Arms by Ernest Hemingway, 1929, Scribner

Chapter Three by Sharlet Mentes

1. *The Zen Path Through Depression* by Philip Martin, 2009, HarperOne

2. *Rising Strong: How the Ability to Reset Transforms the Way We Live, Love, Parent, and Lead* by Brené Brown, 2015, Random House

3. *Daring Greatly: How the Courage to Be Vulnerable Transforms the Way We Live, Love, Parent, and Lead* by Brené Brown, 2012, Avery

Chapter Four by Marika Soleil

A Joseph Campbell Companion: Reflections on the Art of Living by Joseph Campbell, 1992, Harper

Chapter Nine by Kate Ikert

Braving the Wilderness: The Quest for True Belonging and the Courage to Stand Alone by Brené Brown, 2017, Random House

THE GCW PUBLISHING HOUSE AND MEDIA GROUP™

GCW PUBLISHING HOUSE

We aren't your average publisher! GCW Publishing House and Media Group™ is a Canadian woman-owned and operated publishing house that ignites courage and confidence in women worldwide and helps them write high-impact, non-fiction books that make waves, move mountains, blaze trails, and change lives! We combine the art of storytelling, connection, camaraderie, support, marketing, and public relations into the book-writing experience to provide our authors with the entire publishing process and beyond!

For more information on publishing, blogging, and podcasting opportunities, please visit: gcwpublishing.com

AVAILABLE NOW

THE SHE SERIES

The Great Canadian Woman is every woman. She is overcoming trauma. She is coming to terms with her intuition. She is changing careers and finding a new path. She is grieving while raising her children. She is overcoming racial injustices. She is removing mental health stigmas. She is finding her joy. She is raw and real. She is a light in the darkness. She stumbles and falls, but she rises by sharing her story and speaking her truth. Sometimes we need to break so we can rebuild. In the chapters of this book, these great Canadian women show you how to do just that through their intense vulnerability, massive strength, immense courage, and endless perseverance.

AVAILABLE NOW

SHE GRIEVES | SHE IS ENOUGH | SHE IS JUST GETTING STARTED

SHE GRIEVES—A special edition of real-life stories written by women who have learned to navigate the tsunami of grief and rise above the storm. A collection that will inspire and give permission to find purpose and joy to those living with grief.

SHE IS ENOUGH—A collection of real-life stories from women who have realized their worth-stories that will encourage all women to trust their intuition and live their life on purpose.

SHE IS JUST GETTING STARTED—A collection of real-life stories from women who chose to step into their power, navigate the world of uncertainty, rewrite the story of what "success" means to them, and embark on their entrepreneurial path—stories that will help inspire future generations of women in their transition to entrepreneurship.

ALSO AVAILABLE

SHE IS WORTHY | SHE LIVES HER TRUTH

SHE IS WORTHY—A collection of real-life stories of women who have overcome hurdles that once bruised their self-esteem, so they could lead their lives with courage and confidence.

SHE LIVES HER TRUTH—A collection of stories and lessons from resilient women on their journey toward trusting their inner knowing and living with intention.

ALSO BY GCW PUBLISHING HOUSE

THE GREAT CANADIAN WOMAN— SHE IS STRONG AND FREE SERIES

An inspiring three-volume series of real-life stories from Canadian women who have overcome life adversities, found a way through seemingly impossible circumstances, and rose above their pain and tribulations. Their courageous stories will instill a sense of hope and empowerment in others so that they, too, can overcome their personal hardships and know they are not alone. These stories grant us all the permission to live fully, love deeply, and fight like hell in the name of happiness.

GCW PUBLISHING HOUSE

Manufactured by Amazon.ca
Acheson, AB

11628902R00035